CW01637802

THE COMPLETE

OWNERS GUIDE

Essential facts tips and information about keeping Vizsla's including; Feeding, Health, Housing, Training, Canine Psychology, Grooming, Breeding and much more.

MARGARET DAVIS

Published by:
KARM Publishing
ISBN: 978-1-910915-07-3

Disclaimer and Legal Notice

The author has made every effort to ensure the accuracy of the information within this book was correct at time of publication. Whilst the author has tried to keep the information up-to-date and correct, there are no representations or warranties, express or implied, about the completeness, accuracy, reliability, suitability or availability with respect to the information, products, services, or related graphics contained in this publication for any purpose. The author does not assume and hereby disclaims any liability to any party for any loss, damage, or disruption caused by errors or omissions, whether such errors or omissions result from accident, negligence, or any other cause.

The methods described within this publication are the author's prior knowledge and/or personal thoughts and/or opinions and/or experience of the subject. They are not intended to be a definitive set of instructions for this subject. Other methods, instructions, opinions and materials may be available to accomplish the same end result. Again under no circumstance can the author/publisher accept legal responsibility or liability for any loss, damage to property and/or personal injury, arising from any error or omissions from the information contained in this publication or from failure of the reader to correctly and precisely follow any information contained within the publication.

3rd party sources/information:

The author/publisher has no control, and is therefore not responsible for the content, availability or nature of any third party websites or other publications listed herein. Access and use of information of third party websites or other publications, is at your own risk. Any website publication or the information listed within them should not be implied as an endorsement or recommendation by the author/publisher.

The information provided within this publication, is strictly for educational purposes and general informational purposes only. If you wish to apply ideas contained in this publication, you are taking full responsibility for your actions. Therefore, any use of this information is at your own risk.

Additional Disclaimer and Legal Notice information:

You must not in any circumstances:

a) publish, republish, sell, license, sub-license, rent, transfer, broadcast, distribute or redistribute the publication or any part of the publication;

b) edit, modify, adapt or alter the publication or any part of the publication;

c) use of the publication or any part of the publication in any way that is unlawful or in breach of any person's legal rights under any applicable law, or in any way that is offensive, indecent, discriminatory or otherwise objectionable;

d) use of the publication or any part of the publication to compete with us, whether directly or indirectly; or

e) use the publication or any part of the publication for a commercial purpose

(1) No advice

The publication contains information about Vizsla dogs. The information is not advice, and should not be treated as such. You must not rely on the information in the publication as an alternative to (legal/medical/veterinary/ financial/accountancy or other relevant) advice from an appropriately qualified professional. If you have any specific questions about any (legal/medical /veterinary/ financial/accountancy or other relevant) matter you should consult an appropriately qualified professional.

(2) Limited Warranties

We do not warrant or represent that the use of the publication will lead to any particular outcome or result.

(3) Limitations and exclusions of liability

We will not be liable to you in respect of any business losses, including (without limitation) loss of or damage to profits, income, revenue, use, production, anticipated savings, business, contracts, commercial opportunities or goodwill.

We will not be liable to you in respect of any loss or corruption of any data, database, hardware or software. We will not be liable to you in respect of any special, indirect or consequential loss or damage.

(4) Trademarks

Registered and unregistered trademarks or service marks in the publication are the property of their respective owners. Unless stated otherwise, we do not endorse and are not affiliated with any of the holders of any such rights and as such we cannot grant any licence to exercise such rights.

About the Author;

Margaret Davis; has been involved with animals her whole life. Dogs in particular have been a passion of hers. She has been blessed over the years with many four legged friends. She considers it an absolute privilege and labour of love to be involved in this publication.

Acknowledgements

As for work put into the creation of this book I would like to thank my parents and family for their perpetual love and support. And with a special sweetness, my canine friends past and present, who have taught me the true meaning of friendship, devotion and loyalty, to name but a few of their fabulous traits. Their constant love, positivity and enthusiasm for life is truly inspiring.

Table of Contents

Author Note

If you are reading this information as an experienced dog owner, then parts such as the glossary will already be familiar to you. Having said that, the information is intended for everyone and I am sure that even the experienced dog person will find a lot of new facts and information.

It is not my intention to patronize the reader and to tell you how you should read a book. However, unless you are an experienced dog person and are confident enough to skip certain sections, I would highly recommend that you thoroughly read all of the contents before you begin to implement any of the instructions. You may wish to take notes as you go or re-read the book a second time noting important steps to give yourself an action plan.

Also, please note that the use of pronouns like 'his', 'him' or 'her' throughout the text, is simply for ease of reading. It is generally intended to refer to both sexes. It is not meant to indicate a preference by the author of one sex over the other.

Introduction

The Vizsla is a Hungarian sporting dog known for its graceful appearance, hunting ability, and beautiful reddish brown coat. These medium-sized dogs are treasured for their intelligence and train-ability, but they are also very gentle and loyal which makes them excellent family pets. The Vizsla is a very healthy and hearty breed that has been kept by hunters and families for more than a thousand years. If you are looking for a loyal, affectionate, and loving breed then the Vizsla might be the right choice for you.

If you are considering the Vizsla breed, this book is the perfect place to start. In this book you will find all of the information you need to know in order to decide whether the Vizsla is the right breed for you. Not only will you learn the basics about owning and raising dogs, but you will also receive breed-specific tips for feeding, training, and caring for your Vizsla. By the time you finish this book you will be fully equipped with the knowledge you need to be the best Vizsla owner you can be.

You may be familiar with the glossary of a book appearing towards the end. However, it is included here in the beginning to familiarise and briefly introduce some common terms and themes throughout the book. Hopefully this will enhance your reading enjoyment from the beginning.

Glossary of Terms

* ***AKC*** – American Kennel Club, the largest purebred dog registry in the United States

* ***Balance*** – A show term referring to all of the parts of the dog, both moving and standing, which produce a harmonious image

* ***Beard*** – Long, thick hair on the dog's underjaw

* ***Best in Show*** – An award given to the only undefeated dog left standing at the end of judging

* ***Bitch*** – A female dog

* ***Bite*** – The position of the upper and lower teeth when the dog's jaws are closed; positions include level, undershot, scissors, or overshot

* ***Board*** – To house, feed, and care for a dog for a fee

* ***Breed*** – A domestic race of dogs having a common gene pool and characterized appearance/function

* ***Breed Standard*** – A published document describing the look, movement, and behavior of the perfect specimen of a particular breed

* ***Clip*** – A method of trimming the coat in some breeds

* ***Coat*** – The hair covering of a dog; some breeds have two coats; an outer coat and undercoat, also known as a double coat. Examples of breeds with double coats include German Shepherd, Siberian Husky, Akita, etc.

* ***Condition*** – The health of the dog as shown by its skin, coat, behavior, and general appearance

* ***Crate*** – A container used to house and transport dogs; also called a cage or kennel

* ***Dam (bitch)*** – The female parent of a dog.

* ***Dock*** – To shorten the tail of a dog by surgically removing the end part of the tail.

* ***Double Coat*** – Having an outer weather-resistant coat and a soft, waterproof coat for warmth; see ***Coat***.

* ***Drop Ear*** – An ear in which the tip of the ear folds over and hangs down; not prick or erect

* ***Entropion*** – A genetic disorder resulting in the upper or lower eyelid turning in

* ***Fancier*** – A person who is especially interested in a particular breed or dog sport

* ***Groom*** – To brush, trim, comb or otherwise make a dog's coat neat in appearance

* ***Heel*** – To command a dog to stay close by its owner's side

* ***Hip Dysplasia*** – A condition characterized by the abnormal formation of the hip joint

* ***Inbreeding*** – The breeding of two closely related dogs of one breed

* ***Kennel*** – A building or enclosure where dogs are kept

* ***Litter*** – A group of puppies born at one time

* ***Markings*** – A contrasting color or pattern on a dog's coat

* ***Mask*** – Dark shading on the dog's foreface

* ***Mate*** – To breed a dog and a bitch

* ***Neuter*** – To castrate a male dog or spay a female dog

* ***Pads*** – The tough, shock-absorbent skin on the bottom of a dog's foot

* ***Pedigree*** – The written record of a dog's genealogy going back three generations or more

* ***Prick Ear*** – Ear that is carried erect, usually pointed at the tip of the ear

* ***Puppy*** – A dog under 12 months of age

* ***Purebred*** – A dog whose sire and dam belong to the same breed and who are of unmixed descent

* ***Self Color*** – Having one color or whole color except for light-colored shading

* ***Shedding*** – The natural process whereby old hair falls off the dog's body as it is replaced by new hair growth.

* ***Sire*** – The male parent of a dog

* ***Smooth Coat*** – Short hair that is close-lying

* ***Spay*** – The surgery to remove a female dog's ovaries, rendering her incapable of breeding

* ***Trim*** – To groom a dog's coat by plucking or clipping (plucking is often used in wire-haired dogs such as certain types of Vizsla)

* ***Undercoat*** – The soft, short coat typically concealed by a longer outer coat

* ***Wean*** – The process through which puppies transition from subsisting on their mother's milk to eating solid food

* ***Whelping*** – The act of birthing a litter of puppies

Chapter One:

Understanding Vizslas

In order to make an educated decision regarding whether or not the Vizsla is the right breed for you, you need to take the time to learn as much as you can about this wonderful breed. In this chapter you will learn the basics about the Vizsla breed including key facts and a breed history. You will also learn about the cousin to the Vizsla, the Wirehaired Vizsla. After reviewing the information in this chapter you should have a better idea whether or not the Vizsla is the right dog for you and your family.

1.) What are Vizsla Dogs?

The Vizsla is a Hungarian hunting dog known for its sleek appearance, impressive endurance, and its beautiful reddish brown coat. These dogs are the ideal sporting breed but they also make very loyal companions. Not only are Vizslas excellent hunters of fowl and upland game, but they are actually one of the smallest pointer-retriever breeds. If you are looking for a talented hunting breed that lives for sport but you do not want a giant dog around the house, the Vizsla might be a good compromise.

This hunting dog is medium-sized in terms of its build, but it packs a great deal of power and stamina into its small frame. The Vizsla is not just known for its hunting prowess but also for its outstanding train-ability. This breed is incredibly intelligent and eager to learn. This is why it performs so well in a variety of dog sports including hunting, agility trials, and obedience. The Vizsla is a lively and well-mannered breed, though it does have strong protective instincts. Out in the field, the Vizsla is fearless and devoted to the hunt, but in the home, he is sensitive and affectionate with family.

Overall, the Vizsla is built for sport but it can be adaptable to a variety of living conditions. As long as the dog gets enough exercise to work off its energy, the Vizsla will be perfectly happy as a family pet. These dogs are actually one of the few sporting breeds that do very well as family pets and companion animals. Most hunting breeds prefer the company of other dogs, but the Vizsla can become very attached to his human companions and he generally gets on well with children.

2.) Facts About Vizsla Dogs

Also known as the Hungarian Vizsla or the Magyar Vizsla, the Vizsla originated in Hungary. This breed belongs to the Sporting Group for the AKC and the Pointer Group (Group 7) for the Federation Cynologique Internationale (FCI). One of the most appealing characteristics of the Vizsla breed is its medium size. Many hounds and pointing breeds are much larger than the Vizsla. In addition to being medium-sized, the Vizsla is gentle and well-mannered in temperament which makes it a great family pet.

Vizsla dogs have short, close-lying coats that are fairly dense, but these dogs do not have a woolly undercoat. Because its coat is so short, and because the undercoat is absent, this breed is not well-suited to living outdoors. Though this dog cannot be kept outside, it is unique among indoor dogs in that it doesn't require a lot of grooming or bathing. The Vizsla is only an average shedder and it is a self-cleaning breed that doesn't require frequent bathing. In fact, the Vizsla does not have the characteristic "dog" smell that many people complain of in other breeds.

In addition to its medium size and hunting prowess, another identifying characteristic of the Vizsla dog breed is its rust-colored coat. The standard coat for the dog breed Vizsla is a solid golden-rust color and it may come in several different shadings. Some describe the Vizsla coat color as copper, russet gold, or dark sandy gold. The only colorations that are considered faults or a disqualification in show are the pale yellow and the solid dark mahogany colorations. Some white markings on the fore-chest, tail, and neck are allowed but not preferred. The color of the Vizsla's eyes, nose and nails usually blend with the coat.

In terms of its size, the male Vizsla stands about 22 to 25 inches (56-64 cm) tall and the average male Vizsla weight is between 45 and 66 lbs. (20 to 30 kg). The female Vizsla size is about 21 to 24 inches (53 to 61 cm) tall and weighs 40 to 55 lbs. (18 to 25 kg) at maturity. The Vizsla has a very long natural tail but the American breed standard calls for it to be docked at two-thirds the original length. Tail docking is banned in several countries so Vizslas in areas like the UK do not have this same requirement. As the Vizsla tracks game, it holds its tail perpendicular to the ground, wagging it vigorously as it runs. The Vizsla's tail is much longer than the tails of other docked breeds such as the Boxer, Weimaraner, and the Doberman. There is some variation in tail length among Vizslas because docking is usually performed at 3 days after birth.

As noted previously the Vizsla is usually a gentle and well-mannered breed. While many hounds and pointers prefer the company of other dogs and do not form strong bonds with their owners, the Vizsla makes an excellent family pet and companion. These dogs want to spend as much time with their owners as possible. The Vizsla thrives on exercise and human interaction which contributes to this breed's success as a household pet. Sometimes the Vizsla is nicknamed the "Velcro dog" because of their tendency to stick close to their owners.

The Vizsla has very strong protective instincts and he may be wary around strangers, particularly if he thinks they may be a threat to the family, his "pack". These dogs can be trained as guard dogs because they do not hesitate to bark at intruders on their perceived territory. This breed is also excellent at various dog sports because it is very intelligent and trainable. One thing to be wary of with this breed is that it can become whiny or develop behavior problems if it doesn't get enough attention or exercise. Vizsla puppies should begin training and socialization as early as possible, and you should maintain a firm and consistent hand in training.

For the most part, the Vizsla is a healthy breed and it has an average lifespan between 10 and 14 years. Though the Vizsla lifespan is fairly long, there are a few heritable conditions to which the breed is prone. Vizslas are at-risk of developing hip dysplasia, canine epilepsy, lymphoma, hemangiosarcoma, and sebaceous adenitis. Responsible breeding practices can help to reduce the risk for these disease in Vizsla puppies. Having your dog seen regularly by a veterinarian and making sure he stays up to date on vaccinations will also help to ensure his health.

Summary of Vizsla Facts

* Pedigree: ancestors were hunting dogs of the Magyar tribes living in the Carpathian Basin during the 10th century

Vizsla Facts!

* *Height (male)*: 22 to 25 inches (56-64 cm)

* *Height (female)*: 21 to 24 inches (53 to 61 cm)

* *Weight (male)*: 45 to 66 lbs. (20 to 30 kg)

* *Weight (female)*: 40 to 55 lbs. (18 to 25 kg)

* *Coat Length*: short and close-lying

* *Coat Texture*: smooth and dense; no woolly undercoat (obviously relatively rough coated with the wirehaired type.)

* *Color*: solid golden-rust; dark mahogany or pale yellow are considered faults

* *Ears*: drop ears; very thin leather

* *Temperament*: high-energy, loyal, well-mannered, affectionate and intelligent.

* *Training*: intelligent and extremely trainable

* *Markings*: some small white markings on the forehead, chest, neck, and tail are permissible

* *Eyes and Nose*: reddish; eye, nose, and nail color should blend with the coat color

* *Tail*: very long; usually docked at two-thirds length

* *Exercise Needs*: fairly high; long daily walk or jog recommended; breed is likely to develop problem behaviors without adequate mental/physical stimulation

* *Lifespan*: average 10 to 14 years

* *Health Conditions*: hip dysplasia, canine epilepsy, lymphoma, hemangiosarcoma, and sebaceous adenitis

3.) Vizsla Breed History

The exact origins of the Vizsla are unknown because it is a very old breed. It is hypothesized, however, that the ancestors of the breed were native dogs used for hunting by the Magyar tribes that lived in the Carpathian Basin during the 10th century. There are primitive stone etchings dated more than a thousand years showing Magyar hunters with both his falcon and his Vizsla dog. The first written reference to the breed didn't occur until 1357. It was recorded in the ***Illustrated Vienna Chronicle*** by the Carmelite Friars.

For many centuries, the Vizsla was prized as a companion dog by barons and warlords. As a result, the bloodline was preserved and kept pure by the aristocracy who guarded the breed jealously. In addition to preserving the bloodline of Vizslas, the aristocracy also helped to develop the breed's hunting abilities. The popularity of the breed helped it to survive the Turkish occupation lasting from 1526 to 1696 and the Hungarian Revolution between 1848 and 1849. The breed stayed strong through two World Wars and the Soviet Period.

During the 1800s and early 1900s however, the breed faced several near-extinctions. After World War II, breed fanciers sought out Vizslas of the true type and used them to revive the breed. At the close of World War II, the Vizsla was brought to the United States for the first time. Here, its popularity continued to rise and the Vizsla Club of America was formed in the 1950s. The Vizsla remains one of the top 50 breeds in the UK with about 1,000 puppies being registered with the Kennel Club each year. A Vizsla even won Best-in-Show at the 2010 Crufts show.

A.) The Vizsla Club of America

The Vizsla Club of America (VCA) was formed in the early 1950s, started by a group of Vizsla fanciers. Originally, the club went by the name Magyar Vizsla Club but it was renamed The Vizsla Club of America a few years later. In 1953, the VCA started sending out a newsletter to Vizsla lovers, helping to keep them informed about developments with the breed and to keep them connected with each other. In 1960, the Vizsla was formally recognized by the AKC. It was the 115th breed to be recognized.

Every year, 35 regional Vizsla clubs put on a number of shows, rallies, trials, and AKC hunt tests. Each year, the VCA puts on a number of national events including:

* National Field Championship

* Amateur Field Championship

* National Gun Dog Championship

* National Specialty Show (obedience trial, agility trial, rally trial, etc.)

For many years, the VCA has also promoted the versatile nature of the Vizsla breed. In 1981, the club began offering the Versatility Certificate program which recognizes specimens of the breed that meet certain requirements in conformation, field, and obedience. The VCA continues to work for the betterment of the breed, acting in conjunction with the AKC to sponsor health research initiatives, specifically for diseases affecting the Vizsla like lymphoma, epilepsy, brucella, and hemangiosarcoma.

4.) THE WIREHAIRED VIZSLA

The Wirehaired Vizsla is a cousin to the Vizsla but it is considered a completely separate breed by the AKC, the FCI, and other dog breed governing bodies. This dog is very similar in appearance to the Vizsla except for its coat. While the Vizsla has a short, close-lying coat the Wirehaired Vizsla has a slightly longer but equally dense coat. What makes the coat of this breed different from the Vizsla's is its wiry texture. The Wirehaired Vizsla also has a water-repellent undercoat, but the Vizsla does not.

The Wirehaired Vizsla is still a medium-sized hunting dog known for its endurance, well-developed protective instincts, its hunting prowess, and its train-ability. Like the Vizsla, this breed also originated in Hungary where it is used for hunting and kept as a family pet. The Wirehaired Vizsla was only developed during the 1930s and it is still very rare, with only about 30 litters being registered each year. This breed was initially developed by kennel owners Vasas Jozsef and Gresznarik Laszlo. These men sought to produce a dog that exhibited the rich color of the Vizsla but with a heavier coat and more substantial frame to make it more suitable for retrieving from icy water and working in the cold.

In order to achieve their goals, Jozsef and Lazslo bred two Vizsla bitches with a liver-colored German Wirehaired Pointer named Astor von Potat. The best offspring from the pairing were then bred together to produce the first Wirehaired Vizsla litter. Dia de Selle was the first Wirehaired Vizsla to be exhibited. She had the body of a Vizsla with the head of a German Wirehaired Pointer. Though her coat was not as thick as Jozsef and Lazslo intended, it was a step in the right direction. Subsequent breedings resulted in what is now known as the Wirehaired Vizsla.

The Wirehaired Vizsla is remarkably similar to the Vizsla in terms of its appearance, hunting abilities and temperament. The main differences between the breeds are related to the Wirehaired Vizsla's ability to withstand

cold weather. The Wirehaired Vizsla is a medium-sized breed with males standing between 23 to 25 inches (58-64 cm) and weighing between 45 to 66 lbs. (20 to 30 kg). Females of the breed stand about 21.5 to 23 inches (55 to 58 cm) tall and weigh 40 to 55 lbs. (18 to 25 kg). Like the Vizsla, the Wirehaired Vizsla exhibits a uniform rust coloration with its nose, eyes, nails, and lips blending with the coat coloration.

Though both the Vizsla and the Wirehaired Vizsla have a short rust-colored coat, the Wirehaired Vizsla has more pronounced eyebrows and a harsh beard on either side of the muzzle that grows between 0.75 and 1.25 inches (1.9 to 3.2 cm) long. Also similar to the Vizsla, this breed's tail is commonly docked at two-thirds length. The Wirehaired Vizsla still has a lean, muscular build but it is a little more robust than the Vizsla.

In terms of temperament, the Vizsla and the Wirehaired Vizsla are very similar. The Wirehaired Vizsla's main strengths lie in his hunting ability and his natural instincts. Still, this dog is highly trainable for a variety of other dog sports and he makes a great family pet. The Wirehaired Vizsla enjoys spending time with family and he generally gets along well with children. This breed loves to spend as much time with people as possible and may develop problem behaviors or separation anxiety if left alone for long periods of time. This breed is also very active and requires a good deal of daily exercise.

SUMMARY OF WIREHAIRED VIZSLA FACTS

Summary!

* ***Pedigree***: Vizsla bred with German Wirehaired Pointer

* ***Origins***: originally developed in the 1930s

* ***Breed Size***: medium

* ***Height (male)***: 23 to 25 inches (58-64 cm)

* ***Height (female):*** 21 to 24 inches (53 to 61 cm)

* ***Weight (male)***: 45 to 66 lbs. (20 to 30 kg)

* ***Weight (female):*** 40 to 55 lbs. (18 to 25 kg)

* ***Coat Length***: short, close-lying

* ***Heath Conditions:*** hip dysplasia, canine epilepsy, lymphoma, hemangiosarcoma, and sebaceous adenitis

Summary!

* *Coat Texture*: wiry and dense; water-repellent undercoat

* *Color*: solid golden-rust; uniform in color

* *Markings*: some small white markings on the forehead, chest, neck, and tail are permissible

* *Face*: pronounced eyebrows and a harsh beard on either side of the muzzle that grows between 0.75 and 1.25 inches (1.9 to 3.2 cm) long

* *Eyes and Nose*: reddish; eye, nose, and nail color should blend with the coat color

* *Ears*: drop ears; very thin leather

* *Tail*: very long; usually docked at two-thirds length

* *Training*: intelligent and extremely trainable

* *Lifespan:* average 10 to 14 years

* *Exercise Needs*: fairly high; long daily walk or jog recommended; breed is likely to develop problem behaviors without adequate mental/physical stimulation

* *Temperament*: high-energy, loyal, well-mannered, affectionate and intelligent.

Chapter Two:

What to Know Before Buying

Now that you know the basics about the Vizsla breed, you may have a better idea whether or not this is the right dog for you. If you think that it might be, you still have more to learn before you decide. In this chapter you will receive an overview of some of the more practical aspects to owning a Vizsla including information about dog licensing, keeping Vizslas with other pets, and the cost of caring for a Vizsla. You will also receive a list of pros and cons for this particular breed.

1) Do You Need a License?

Becoming a pet owner is a big responsibility, especially if the pet is a dog. Not only do you need to feed and walk your Vizsla, but you also need to take care of some practical responsibilities including licensing your new pet. Before you buy a Vizsla you should take the time to learn whether a license is required in your area and, if so, take the proper steps to obtain one. In this section you will learn about licensing requirements for Vizslas in the United States and in the United Kingdom.

a.) Licensing Vizslas in the U.S.

There are no federal requirements regarding the licensure of dogs in the United States. Rather, these requirements are made at the state level. Before you buy a Vizsla puppy or an adult Vizsla you need to apprise yourself of local dog licensing requirements. Most states require dog owners to license their dogs and, in order to obtain a license, your dog must also be up-to-date on rabies vaccinations. Obtaining a license for your dog is not difficult. Try asking your veterinarian for information or contact your local council instead.

Even if your state does not mandate that you license your dog, it is still a good idea to do it anyway. When you license your dog you will need to provide contact information for yourself. If your dog gets lost and is still carrying his license, whoever finds him will be able to use that information to contact you. Obtaining a dog license requires you to fill out a simple form and to pay a fee around $25 (£16.25). You must renew your license each year, though you may have the option to purchase a five-year license or a lifetime license in some states.

b.) Licensing Vizslas in the U.K.

Licensing requirements for dogs in the U.K. are a little different than they are in the U.S. The U.K. Dog licensing in the UK was abolished in 1987. However, licensing is still mandatory in Northern Ireland, and you can find further details from the website link at the end of the paragraph. Northern Ireland mandates that all dogs carry a license, and the only exception is for assistance dogs and police dogs. Vizsla puppies may be able to get away without a license until they are 6 months old as long as the owner of the puppies is the owner of the mother as well. Dog licenses are renewable annually, just like U.S. licenses. For further information regarding licenses please consult the following link: ***http://www.nidirect.gov.uk/dog-licensing***

2.) How Many Vizslas Should You Keep

Do you get one or two Vizsla dogs. In a lot of cases this is not necessarily breed specific and can often be down to the personality of the dog. Some dogs are quite solitary whereas some require constant companionship. Please therefore consider the following section.

People are often tempted to bring home more than one 'small' dog from a litter. This is more common than with big dogs because smaller dogs seem to 'fit' better into the home and we believe that, due to their size, an extra little dog will be no trouble.

It is certainly true that dogs are social creatures and choose to be around each other. You only need to see the way that the dog seeks others out whilst on walks to see this.

In the wild, dogs live in family groups, feral dogs choose the individuals that they want to spend time and mate with whilst a completely natural wolf pack is a family group consisting of parents and their young.

A pair of dogs play, interact and bond. A pair of dogs is easier on the conscience because you are not leaving a dog completely alone whilst you are at work or socializing. They have the company of one another; which is a much better option for the dog.

Some shelters are looking to rehome dogs in established pairs, these particular dogs are usually friends and highly bonded with each other. Only one of the pair may be a Vizsla dog whilst some may be two of the same breed. This takes some pressure away from you as the dog owner to meet all of the needs of your dog.

This said, a pair can be difficult to handle if they form a pack like mentality and become reactive on walks and in the home. All dogs have individual personalities so the way that a pair of dogs react will really depend on the nature of each dog. Although Vizslas are generally amiable, friendly dogs, two dogs could develop the pack mentality and become a hustle of growling and barking excitement on walks.

If you are looking at puppies though, taking two from the litter is not usually a good idea if you want to be an integral part of your dog's emotional life. Puppies that are taken from the same litter will be very bonded with each other and as they reach adolescence one of two things can happen;

1. They will only focus on each other making them difficult to train and control.
2. They may begin to compete, causing friction between them.

That said, the pair could just as easily settle down and be happy together but it is important that you are aware of the risks.

If you want two Vizsla dogs because of all of the positive points of a bonded pair then you can either look for a pair in rescue or bring one dog home, spend a few months getting to know the dog, socializing him or her perfectly, then look for another dog to join your family.

This is an approach that will work well with dogs of all ages. You may find that one Vizsla dog and a dog of a different breed get on really well together instead of a pair of the same breed.

Having said all of that, experienced Vizsla owners will tell you that this is a very high-maintenance breed. The Vizsla has a friendly personality and an even temperament but they require a lot of attention and exercise. Raising one Vizsla puppy can take a lot of time and energy, so you should think carefully before bringing home two of them. Don't forget, the Vizsla is a very social breed but he tends to prefer the company of people to that of other dogs.

Your Vizsla will form a very strong bond with you and he will want to follow you around the house, getting as much attention as you are willing to give. If you work a full-time job and are not home a lot during the day, the Vizsla might not be the right breed for you. Having a second dog to keep your Vizsla company might help but it will not be a substitute for the level of human interaction this breed craves.

3.) Do Vizslas Get Along with Other Pets

Even though the Vizsla is typically used for hunting and has very well-developed protective instincts, he usually gets along well with other household pets and with children. This breed is primarily used for fowl and upland game hunting, so it may retain a tendency to view pet birds as prey, but other household pets should not be a problem. In order to ensure that your Vizsla gets along with other pets, dogs, and children you should socialize your puppy from an early age. Raising your Vizsla around other pets will help to make sure he gets along with them.

4) A Boy or a Girl

Should you bring home a male or female Vizsla?

This is a question that gets asked a lot. There is however no definitive answer to this but personal preference, particularly if you are going to neuter the dog.

With all of the dogs that I have worked with over the years I never found a preference between sexes. In the last ten years or so we have increasingly learned that dogs have personality; each animal is an individual with distinct traits and preferences.

Therefore a male and a female dog have far more aspects than just their sex. They are all different.

Un-neutered, the male Vizsla will be more likely to develop secondary sexual behavior such as mounting, scent marking and challenging behavior in everyday life, due to the testosterone. The un-neutered female has far less of this behavior type but she may suffer with phantom pregnancies.

Neutering between the two is quite a different procedure. The operation for male dogs is less invasive than for females. Otherwise the choice of sex really is up to you, there is little difference between the two.

5.) Ease and Cost of Care

In addition to thinking about the previously mentioned aspects relating to the Vizsla, you also need to think about the costs associated with keeping a Vizsla. Owning a dog is a big responsibility and there are many costs associated with dog ownership. Not only do you need to provide your Vizsla with shelter, but necessary costs also include food, veterinary care, grooming, and exercise. Before you decide to buy a Vizsla dog you should consider the costs associated with keeping a dog and make sure that you can cover them. In this section you will find a list of initial costs and monthly costs associated with Vizsla ownership as well as an overview and explanation of each.

a.) Initial Costs

The initial costs of owning a Vizsla include those costs you must cover to purchase your dog and to prepare your home for his/her arrival. Initial costs include the purchase price, a crate or kennel, spay/neuter surgery, vaccinations, micro-chipping, and other accessories. Below you will find an overview of each expense as well as an estimated

Initial Costs for Vizsla Dogs

Cost	One Dog	Two Dogs
Purchase Price	$900 to $1,200 (£585 to £780	$1,800 to $2,400 (£1,170 to £1,560)
Crate or Kennel	$35 (£22.75)	$70 (£45.50)
Spay/Neuter	$50 to $200 (£32.50 to £130)	$100 to $400 (£65 to £260)
Vaccinations	$50 (£32.50)	$100 (£65)
Micro-chipping	$15 to $50 (£9.75 to £32.50)	$30 to $100 (£19.50 to £65)
Accessories	$100 (£65)	$200 (£130)
Total	$1,150 to $1,635 (£747.50 to £1,063)	$2,300 to $3,270 (£1,495 to £2,126)

*These rates are based on a conversion rate of $1 U.S. to £0.65 U.K. Rates are subject to change.

cost range:

Purchase Price – The purchase price for Vizsla puppies may vary from one Vizsla breeder to another. Choosing a responsible breeder is incredibly important for Vizslas to minimize the risk of inherited disease. You might be able to find a Vizsla puppy from a hobby breeder for a few hundred $s (£s) but you may not get a good health guarantee. Buying from a responsible breeder will be more expensive, but well worth it in the end. You should expect to find Vizsla puppies for sale from a reputable breeder for about $900 to $1,200 (£585 - £780).

Crate or Kennel – Having a crate or kennel for your Vizsla puppy is very important. Not only will it be instrumental in house-training, but it will give your puppy a place of his own in the house where he can retreat if he wants a nap or just needs a break from people. You will need to upgrade your puppy's crate as he grows but, to start with, a small crate should only cost you about $35 (£22.75) or so.

Spay/Neuter Surgery – Having your Vizsla puppy spayed or neutered is incredibly important, especially if you do not plan to breed your dog. It is recommended that you spay or neuter your puppy before 6 months of age to reduce the risk for certain types of cancer. Spay/neuter surgery can be very expensive if you go to a regular veterinarian but there are plenty of low-cost clinics out there that offer affordable spay/neuter surgery options. If you go to a clinic or shelter, neuter surgery will very likely only cost you $50 to $100 (£32.50 to £65) and spay surgery will generally cost $100 to $200 (£65 to £130).

Vaccinations – Before your Vizsla puppy turns one year old he/she will need to get certain vaccinations. If you buy your puppy from a reputable breeder the pup may already have a few of these vaccinations taken care of by the time you take him home. Speak to your veterinarian about a vaccination schedule for your puppy and plan to spend more or less $50 (£32.50) for your puppy's initial vaccinations.

Micro-chipping – Not only do you need to have your puppy licensed, but you should also consider micro-chipping as well. A dog license is worn on a collar around your dog's neck but a microchip is implanted underneath the skin so that it cannot be lost. The procedure does not hurt your dog and it only takes a few minutes to complete. You should be able to have it done at your local animal shelter for as little as $15 (£9.75) at a shelter or up to $50 (£32.50) for a veterinarian to do it.

Other Accessories – In addition to your dog's crate, you will also need certain accessories. These accessories will include a food dish, water dish, collar, leash, grooming tools, and toys. What you spend on each of these items is up to you and the cost will vary depending on quality. You should expect to pay about $100 (£65) for these accessories, though you could easily spend $200 (£130) or more if you purchased high-quality or designer items.

B.) Monthly Costs

The monthly costs of owning a Vizsla include those recurring costs you must cover on a monthly ongoing basis. Monthly costs include the food and treats, veterinary care, grooming, license renewal, and other costs. Below you will find an overview of each expense as well as an estimated cost range:

Food and Treats – Because the Vizsla is a medium-breed dog, your food costs will not be as high as they would for a large-breed dog. Costs may vary depending on what kind of food you buy, but it is not recommended that you shop by price. The quality of the food you give your dog has a direct impact on his health and wellbeing, so do not skimp. Because the Vizsla is a very high-energy breed you should look for an active or working breed formula. You should plan to spend about $30 (£19.50) on a large bag of dog food that will last you about one month. In addition to food, you should budget an extra $10 (£6.50) per month for treats, especially when you are training your dog.

Veterinary Care – In order to keep your Vizsla in good health you should plan to visit the veterinarian about every 6 months. Your Vizsla puppy may need more frequent visits during the first year for vaccinations, but after that, two visits per year will be adequate. You should expect to spend about $40 (£26) per visit which, with two visits per year, averages to about $7 (£4.55) per month.

Grooming – Because the Vizsla has a very short coat you will not need to take him to the groomer's very often. You will be able to do most of the brushing and bathing yourself at home but you still might want to take your Vizsla to the groomer every 4 to 6 months to

Monthly Costs for Vizsla Dogs

Cost	One Dog	Two Dogs
Food and Treats	$40 (£26)	$80 (£52)
Veterinary Care	$7 (£4.55)	$14 (£9.10)
Grooming	$8.30 (£5.40)	$16.60 (£10.80)
License Renewal	$2 (£1.30)	$4 (£2.60)
Other Costs	$15 (£9.75)	$30 (£19.50)
Total	$72 (£47)	$144 (£94)

*These rates are based on a conversion rate of $1 U.S. to £0.65 U.K. Rates are subject to change.

ensure that his coat and skin remains in good health. You should expect to spend about $50 (£32.50) per visit so, with two visits per year, the average monthly cost for grooming evens out to about $8.30 (£5.40) per month.

License Renewal – Having your dog licensed is incredibly important and it is not a major expense. You only need to have your dog's license renewed once a year and it generally costs about $25 (£16.25) which averages to just $2 (£1.30) per month.

Other Costs – In addition to veterinary care and grooming costs, there are other costs which you may need to cover once in a while. These costs may include new toys, replacement collars as your Vizsla grows, new grooming tools, cleaning products, and more. To be safe, you should budget about $15 (£9.75) per month for these additional costs.

Part of being a responsible dog owner is meeting the needs of your dog. If you cannot comfortably cover the initial costs and ongoing monthly costs described in this section you should not purchase a Vizsla dog.

6.) Pros and Cons for Vizslas Dogs

Vizslas are excellent hunting dogs and they make great pets, but they are not the right choice for everyone. In addition to considering the costs of keeping a Vizsla you should also think about the pros and cons of the breed.

You will find a list of pros and cons for Vizsla dogs listed below:

Pros for Vizsla Dogs

Pros!

* Medium-sized breed, does not need a large amount of space (fenced yard is recommended).

* Short coat does not require a great deal of grooming.

* Only an average shedder.

* Friendly breed by nature; gets along well with people and children.

* Will form strong bonds with family – has well-developed protective instincts.

* Excellent hunting dog; can also be trained for other dog sports

* Usually gets along well with other dogs and pets

* Very intellegent and responsive to training

Cons for Vizsla Dogs

Cons!

* Very active dog – requires a good deal of daily exercise to work off its energy.

* Can be very high-energy in the home – prone to developing destructive behavior without adequate mental/physical stimulation.

* Prone to developing separation anxiety if left alone for long periods of time.

* Socialization is incredibly important to ensure positive interactions with other people and animals.

* High-maintenance breed – requires a lot of human interaction and affection.

Chapter Three:

Purchasing Vizsla Dogs

After learning the basics about the Vizsla breed as well as some practical information you may be ready to decide whether or not the Vizsla is the right pet for you. If it is, the information in this chapter will help you to figure out where to buy Vizsla puppies. Buying a Vizsla puppy is not necessarily as simple as stopping in to your local pet store. You need to be very careful about where you buy your puppy to ensure that it will be healthy. In this chapter you will receive tips for selecting a reputable breeder and for picking a healthy Vizsla puppy out of a litter.

1.) Ethical Vizsla Breeders

There are a few things to consider when buying a Vizsla puppy and if you carry out careful research right at the start then you can be sure that you bring home the right dog for you.

There are many good reasons for choosing a puppy carefully, most of which people are generally unaware. It's easy for us to be trusting of breeders and those that sell puppies but in actual fact dog breeders need to be chosen extra carefully for the following reasons;

* Puppy genetic background.
* Puppy health.
* Puppy social skills.
* Welfare of the puppy parents.

Irresponsible breeding is the main reason for unwanted and sick dogs in the Western world today.

When genetic testing is not carried out; the temperament of the parent dogs is not considered; and if the puppy is not socialized from as early as birth then the dog may well have problems.

If you buy a puppy from an irresponsible breeder, the dog is at risk of health or behavioral problems, or maybe even both, at any time in his life.

The only dog breeder to consider is the one that has a conscience. This is the type that loves the breed and only breeds one or two litters. They will also carry out all of the testing required before making a decision to breed a litter. This type of breeder knows about puppy socialization, about genetic health, and dog welfare is at the forefront of their minds.

The good dog breeder has a list of people wanting the puppies before they even allow the parent dogs to mate. They are extremely interested in finding the correct puppy home, and are not afraid to turn people away.

The good breeder does not have to use classified sites, Facebook or newspapers to advertise their puppies. They are not cagey about the parent dogs and they will always, without fail, allow you to see the puppies with their Mother in the home environment.

You may even feel interviewed, on your initial phone call, by a dog breeder if you are looking for a puppy. If this happens then you can be pretty much certain that you are enquiring about much loved and well-bred Vizsla puppies,

In addition to asking you a lot of questions the good dog breeder will state that they must always be given the option to take the dog back, at any point during its life, if you can no longer care for it. There may even be a contract.

The puppies will be wormed, health checked, vaccinated and at least eight weeks old before they leave their Mother.

2.) Beware of the Puppy Farmer!

The opposite side to the ethical breeder is the 'puppy farmer'. Not everyone with Vizsla puppies for sale is a good and ethical dog breeder. In actual fact some care very little about the dogs in their charge.

This is a trap that most people fall into when looking for a puppy. It's actually hard to believe that people would farm dogs in this way, but it happens and if you are looking for a puppy you can be sure that at least some of your options are puppy farmed dogs.

The pet store puppy is usually from a puppy mill as are those sold in big sized litters through classifieds. This is not to say that buying puppies from classified ads is a bad thing. Some excellent puppies are available this way, and often this is the most convenient way a reputable 'hobby' breeder can find potential puppy parents. Although all puppies look the same, usually healthy, clean, fluffy and with that addictive puppy scent, the farmed puppy is very different indeed.

Soon we will talk in detail about puppy development and how vital it is towards a puppy's overall mental health. This knowledge is equally important to the act of sourcing a puppy. For now, in case you are tempted by the pet store Vizsla puppy it is vital that you know how he got to be "That Doggy in the Window".

The puppy mill is a harrowing place. It is much the same as a factory farm for pigs, cows and chickens. Dogs are kept in small pens and bred from, each time the dog comes into season. The Mother dog is stressed throughout her life and often puppy farmed dogs never go for a walk. They rarely, if at all, receive veterinary attention.

The dogs are kept in small pens and rarely cleaned up after. They are also rarely handled and are fed on cheap food.

As you can probably imagine bacteria thrives in this type of environment and stress levels are high. With the ever increasing link between low quality commercial food and illness, a puppy born and whelped in this type of environment will have a very poor start in life.

Studies are increasingly showing that the presence of stress in a pregnant mother dog can lead to flighty and fearful puppies with the behavior only showing up in the dog's adolescent and adult life.

So how do you recognize a puppy farmer or a puppy that has been bred for money alone?

The signs of a puppy farmer are quite easy to spot when you know what to look for. The important thing to remember with this type of dog breeder is that the most important thing to them is money, and the way that they act will betray this.

Warning signs when deciding on a dog breeder are as follows;

Beware!

* The breeder will have a lot of dogs available and often of different breeds.

* The puppy may be quite cheap.

* There will be no proof of worming, vaccination or veterinary checks.

* Meeting the mother of the puppy will not be possible.

* The breeder will not allow you to see the puppy in the whelping environment.

* The puppy will be younger than eight weeks old when it is sold.

* The breeder will ask very few questions about the home you are offering.

* The breeder will offer to deliver or meet you somewhere with the puppy.

It may be tempting to buy a puppy from this type of breeder anyway and see it as a sort of rescue attempt. This is highly inadvisable because the puppy farmer only exists as a result of people buying their puppies. Therefore to buy a dog in this way is funding the cruel practice of puppy farming. In addition to this, any dog that comes from this type of environment is at high risk of stress based behavior problems developing later.

The risk of genetic and environmental health problems caused by bad care of the parent dogs and their offspring from pregnancy onwards, is greatly increased when buying any puppy from a puppy farmer.

3.) Where to Buy Vizsla Dogs

The Vizsla is still a fairly rare breed in some regions, so purchasing a Vizsla may not be as easy to locate and be as available as some other breeds. If you want to buy a Vizsla puppy your best bet may be to find a reputable breeder. As previously indicated, finding Vizsla breeders is not a task that you should take lightly. You need to find a quality breeder that takes great care to select healthy breeding stock and then raises the puppies properly. If you buy your Vizsla from an inexperienced or hobby breeder, you may end up with a Vizsla that has some kind of congenital de-

fect or other health issues. Having said that, some excellent healthy dogs can be found from these sources. However, health checks and screenings may not be as rigorous as they should be. In this section you will find tips for buying a Vizsla in the U.S. and in the U.K. You will also find information about Vizsla rescue dogs.

A.) Buying in the U.S.

When it comes to buying puppies in the United States you have two main options; a pet store or an independent breeder. Again, unfortunately, many pet stores receive their stock from puppy mills. You already know a puppy mill is a breeding facility where dogs are kept in squalid conditions and forced to breed until they are no longer able; they are then disposed of. The puppies that come from puppy mills may be inbred or bred from unhealthy stock which means that they too are likely to be unhealthy. Buying from a pet store is generally not a good option unless you know exactly where the puppy came from and you can confirm that it is from a reputable breeder.

When you buy a puppy from a reputable breeder you are assured that the breeding stock is in good health. Most reputable breeders put their breeding stock through genetic testing before breeding to ensure that they are not going to pass on congenital conditions like hip dysplasia or progressive retinal atrophy. Responsible breeders also know a lot about the breed and can help you to decide whether it is a good choice for you.

In the next section you will find more detailed information about choosing a reputable breeder. For now, however, you will find a list of U.S. Vizsla breeders below:

This is not a definitive list and I would like to point out; **the author is in no way endorsing or recommending any breeder in particular.** This is for informational purposes only and again, I urge you to do your own research, on these or any other breeder sites.

Mira Vizslas.
http://www.miravizslas.com/

Busch Vizslas.
http://www.buschvizslas.com/

Legacy Vizslas.
http://www.legacyvizslas.net/

Martinsen's Vizslas.
http://www.martinsensvizslas.com/

You may also be able to find Vizsla breeders through the ***Vizsla Club of America breeder directory***:

http://www.vcaweb.org/breeder_dir/display_dir.php

B.) Buying in the U.K.

Purchasing Vizsla puppies in the U.K. is very similar to buying them in the U.S. Always do your research before buying Vizsla puppies in the U.K. to ensure that the Vizslas for sale have been bred properly. The last thing you want is to pay for a puppy from a breeder just to find that it is unhealthy. Below you will find a list of breeders with Vizsla puppies for sale U.K.

Again, this is not a definitive list and I would like to point out; **the author is in no way endorsing or recommending any breeder in particular.** This is for informational purposes only and again, I urge you to do your own research, on these or any other breeder sites.

Gunfield Hungarian Vizslas.
http://hungarianvizsla.org.

uk/home.htm

Pitswarren Hungarian Vizslas.
http://www.pitswarren.co.uk/

Hampshire Vizslas.
http://www.hampshirevizslas.com/2015/

Sustead Viszlas.
http://susteadvizslas.co.uk/

You may also be able to find Vizsla breeders through the ***UK Kennel Club Vizsla breeder directory***:
http://www.thekennelclub.org.uk/

Or the ***Hungarian Vizsla Club breeder directory:***

http://www.hungarianvizslaclub.org.uk/puppies-available/

C. Adopting a Rescue Dog

Unless you specifically have your heart set on a Vizsla puppy, you may be able to find an adult Vizsla at a local animal shelter or Vizsla rescue. There are many benefits to adopting an adult dog versus buying a puppy. For one thing, adopting prices are much lower than the cost of purchasing a puppy from a breeder. Adoption rates typically range from $100 to $200 (£65 to £130). Furthermore, when you adopt an adult dog it may already be house-trained and have had some obedience training.

While raising a puppy is great, it can take a lot of time and commitment and it can be a challenge. If you do not want to deal with a puppy having accidents in your house or if you want to avoid the whole teething stage, adopting an adult dog may be the right choice. Furthermore, when you buy a puppy from a Vizsla breeder you do not know what its temperament and personality will be when it grows up. If you adopt an adult dog, what you see is what you get.

If you are thinking of adopting a Vizsla rescue dog, consider one of the rescues or shelters:

Utah/Idaho Vizsla Rescue, Inc.
http://www.utahvizsla.org/>

Midwest Vizsla Rescue.
http://www.midwestvizslarescue.org/

New Hope Vizsla Rescue.
http://www.newhopevizslarescue.org/

You can also find information about local Vizsla shelters through the ***VCA rescue contact list:***
http://vcaweb.org/rescue/contacts.shtml

Hungarian Vizsla Welfare Charity.
http://hungarianvizslawelfare.org.uk/

Hungarian Vizsla Society Rescue.
http://www.vizsla.org.uk/rescue.html

4.) Fostering

Fostering is an excellent option if you are unsure about whether you can commit to looking after a dog on a permanent basis.

The purpose of fostering and adopting dogs and other animals is to prevent euthanasia. Fostering can also provide better alternatives for all animals, by providing a safe and nurturing temporary home. Fostering also increases the live-release rate of all pets, and reduces the number of dogs and cats that die from homelessness. Many rescue groups rely on foster homes to do their great work. These rescue groups will also at times end up paying for dogs to board at kennels when they do not have enough foster homes to turn to.

Fostering entails a temporary arrangement of a limited time where a person takes care of a dog, until a permanent home can be found for that dog. It is not adopting. However, quite often, many foster parents will end up adopting the dog that they foster.

A) Vizsla Fostering

This is an arrangement between a shelter or a Vizsla rescue group and the person agreeing to foster. In this case there will be a contract between you and the Vizsla rescue group, detailing the responsibilities between both parties such as whom is responsible for veterinary bills, training, transport and food.

B) Questions To Ask Before Fostering a Vizsla

It is very likely that the rescue center organizing the fostering would answer all of these and more anyway. But it is good for you to be aware of the type of issues you will face.

* Who pays the veterinary bills? Would that include all veterinary treatments?

* Is my foster Vizsla currently on any medication, or in need of ongoing treatment?

* Do I speak with potential adopters, screening them and possibly introducing my Vizsla to them?

* Will I be required to bring my foster Vizsla to certain adoption events and if so, how many times a month?

* Does the Vizsla have any behavioral issues that require training, and can you provide this? Can I choose my own trainer?

* Do I get to keep him permanently?

* Who pays for dog food, veterinary supplies and dog training supplies? This is likely to be you but is worth asking as some may be available via the center.

* If my foster Vizsla has any behavioral problems, whom can I contact?

* How long will I be fostering this Vizsla?

* What happens should I change my mind, or if I'm not a good fit?

* What should I do if my foster Vizsla does not get along with my other pets?

5.) Choosing a Reputable Breeder

Once you have decided that the Vizsla is the right breed for you, you must take on the task of choosing a reputable breeder. Not only do you need to do some research, such as the recommended breeders above, to find a good breeder, but you also need to speak to the different breeders to determine which breeder is the best. As previously mentioned, the responsible Vizsla breeder will be careful about selecting healthy breeding stock and they will keep detailed records of their breeding practices. If the breeder does not appear to be experienced with the Vizsla breed, or with breeding dogs in general, you should look elsewhere.

In addition to the above recommendations, try asking around at your local animal shelter or a veterinarian's office for their recommendations. Because the Vizsla is rapidly becoming a popular breed (it was ranked 33rd in AKC registration statistics in 2014) there may be a breeder in your area that you do not know about. If neither of these options turns up any breeders, try looking in the phone book or perform an additional online search. Once you have compiled a list of several breeders, you can then go through the list to determine which one is the best option.

Follow the steps below to choose a reputable Vizsla breeder:

Advisable!

* Visit the website for each breeder, if they have one, and look for important information such as photos of the facilities, the breeder's experience, and a license from the Vizsla Club of America.

* Contact each breeder by phone and ask them questions about their experience with breeding and with Vizslas. If the breeder is hesitant to answer your questions, or if they do not seem knowledgeable and experienced, move on to the next option.

* Evaluate the breeder's interest in learning more about you. A reputable breeder will not just sell his puppies to anyone, they should be eager to ask you questions to see if you are a good fit for one of their puppies.

* Narrow your list down to two or three breeders that seem to be a good fit and visit the facilities before you make a commitment to buy a puppy.

* Ask for a tour of the facilities and look to make sure that the dogs are kept in clean conditions and that they appear to be in good health.

* Make sure you see the breeding stock for the puppies that are available to make sure that they are in good health and purebred specimens of the Vizsla breed.

* Ask to see the puppies that are available and make sure that they are kept in clean conditions. Remember, if they are under 6 weeks of age, the puppies should be kept with the mother.

* Choose the breeder that you feel is most knowledgeable and experienced, as well as the one that has puppies available. You will also probably get a gut feeling as to whether they are a reputable breeder or not.

* Ask about the process for reserving a puppy. You will probably have to leave a deposit by way of a down payment. In addition, ask what comes with the puppy (inoculations, worming etc).

* A reputable breeder will offer some kind of health guarantee on the puppy as well as information about the parents to certify its breeding.

6.) Selecting a Healthy Vizsla Puppy

After you have gone through the process of selecting a reputable Vizsla breeder, your next step is to choose a healthy puppy. Whilst it may be tempting to buy the first Vizsla puppy that comes up to you with a wagging tail, you need to be a little more cautious about the process. Taking the time to ensure that the puppy is in good health could save you a lot of veterinary bills (not to mention heartache) in the future.

<u>Follow the steps on the next page to pick a healthy Vizsla puppy:</u>

1. Ask to see all of the puppies at once and spend a few minutes watching how they interact with each other before you approach them.

2. Healthy puppies should be playful and energetic, and should not be acting lethargic.

3. Make yourself available to the puppies, but do not immediately try to interact. Wait and see which ones are curious enough to approach you.

4. Vizsla puppies are very energetic and playful, so they should be eager to interact with you.

5. Spend a few minutes engaging with each puppy. Play with a toy to gauge the puppy's activity and try petting him to make sure he doesn't respond with fear or aggression.

6. If you can, watch the puppies being fed to make sure that they have a healthy appetite. A puppy that does not eat is likely to be sick.

7. Examine the puppies more closely for signs of good health. Do not just look for obvious signs of illness.

Below is a list of what you should look for in different categories when choosing your healthy puppy:

Important!

* ***Eyes***: bright and clear; no discharge or crust

* ***Breathing***: quiet and steady; no snorting, coughing, or sneezing

* ***Energy***: alert and energetic; eager to play

* ***Body***: The puppy should look well-fed, not too skinny

* ***Coat***: the coat should be clean and healthy without bare patches, flaking skin, or other problems; the color should be uniform

* ***Hearing***: the puppy should react if you clap your hands behind his head

* ***Vision***: the puppy should be able to see clearly if you toss a toy or roll a ball across his line of sight

* ***Gait***: the puppy should move easily without limping or evidence of soreness/stiffness

* ***Genitals***: the genitals should be clean

If the puppies appear to be physically healthy and do not show any behavioral warning signs like aggression, excessive fear, or lethargy, then they are probably a good buy. Once you've assessed the condition of the puppies you can spend some more time playing with them to find out which puppy is a good personality match for you. Keep in mind that the personality and temperament of your puppy might change a little as he grows, but you have some control over that depending on how you train and socialize him over the coming weeks.

7.) Naming your puppy

If you have finally chosen the dog or puppy you want then perhaps now is as good a time as any to decide on his name. If you have hopefully bought from a reputable breeder, and are leaving a deposit to then collect him in a few weeks time, then you can ask the breeder to start calling him by that name.

Choosing your dog's name is exciting. Even an adult dog can learn a new name and some have no choice, arriving into rescue nameless.

It is pretty easy to teach your dog his new name and considering how clever this breed is, the process should only take a few days. The idea is simply to show the dog that the sound of a certain word (his name or training command), means that he will need to pay attention, because you are speaking to him.

Eventually your dog will know when he is being talked about just by the sound of his name. For now though, you can offer him treats and say his name, plus call him between two people then use his name as he approaches. I simply say the name, give the dog a small treat and repeat this five or six times each session.

You can also prefix every positive interaction with your dog with his name.

This way he will learn it even quicker.

Never use his name for anything negative or your dog will try his hardest not to respond when he hears it. You certainly do not want your dog to be fearful of hearing his name, because he thinks he has done something wrong. Always make it positive and fun and soon your dog will know exactly who he is.

You probably already have ideas yourself, but if not, please make the name short and sweet. Something like, Daisy, Tess, Max or a name that relates to his appearance such as Patch.

8) PUPPY-PROOFING YOUR HOME

Depending on when you visit the breeder, the puppies may not be ready to take home just yet. As mentioned previously, a responsible breeder will not sell a puppy under 8 weeks old or until the puppies are fully weaned. Even if the puppies are available when you visit you should wait until you have prepared your home before buying the puppy. Below you will find some important steps to take, in puppy-proofing your home:

Your Vizsla will want to explore every nook and cranny of his new home. Part of that process involves his teeth. Keep all items that are valuable or dangerous away from him. This particularly includes electrical cables that may be live and therefore the puppy is risking an electric shock and at worse a fatality. Replace them with non-toxic chew-able puppy toys in bright colors. Any chewed items are your responsibility, and you should be aware that the puppy may see lots of interesting things to chew. They do not see the value or the danger, so please be aware that it is not your Vizsla's fault if something gets chewed. Never use harsh corrections. Not even a tap on the nose. Instead use a firm "No" and replace the item with a chew-able dog toy made especially for teething pups.

Anywhere within your home that your Vizsla puppy is allowed to wander, needs to be puppy proofed. This is similar to baby proofing your home, and requires you to go down on hands and knees and see what dangers lurk at puppy eye level.

Puppies enjoy chewing the solid rubberized covering of electrical cords and outlets. ***BE AWARE***, these can result in your puppy getting a nasty shock, severely burned, or a fatality. Pups can also pull down electrical appliances by yanking on the cords.

Be Aware!

* Prevent your Vizsla from jumping up on any unstable objects like bookcases.

* Do not allow your Vizsla access to high decks or ledges, balconies, open windows, or staircases. Instead use baby gates, baby plastic fencing and therefore prevent accidents from happening.

* Keep your doors securely shut and again prevent a potential accident.

* Never slam doors with a Vizsla puppy in the house. Use doorstops to make sure that the wind does not slam a door in your Vizsla's face.

* Clear glass doors also pose a danger since your Vizsla may not see them and run right into one. Use a screen door.

* Check for toxic plants, medicines, sharp objects, and even dead branches. Your Vizsla puppy could run right into something at break neck speed.

The whole point of the preceding is to get you to think about any potential hazards for your Vizsla. Remember, they are relying on you as their guardian, in much the same way as a child.

A.) Toxins To Be Aware of in Your Home

* Insecticides

* Human medications

* Household cleaning products

* Foods that we consume that have a toxic effect on dogs such as grapes and chocolates

* Rodenticides

* Plants

* Garden and pool products

* Glass, razors, bathroom products

* Coins, small batteries and other small objects that may easily be ingested

You'll need to watch your Vizsla puppy very carefully for the first few months to make sure that he does not get into harms way. Usually the kitchen is made into the puppy's room. In this instance, it's best to make sure that all cleaning supplies are removed and placed elsewhere. Vizsla pups are curious, and it can take as little as a few minutes for your puppy to get into a poisonous cleaning product.

B.) Checking For Toxins in Puppy Toys

Before purchasing toys for your Vizsla to play with, you'll need to check that they are lead free and cadmium free.

Vulnerable puppies are at risk of been given chew toys that may contain lead and cadmium.

Studies from the University of Wisconsin-Madison demonstrate that all toxic responses to environmental pollutants begin to appear in stressed animals. It's important to remove all environmental stressors from your Vizsla's life, and to do all you can to prevent him from being isolated and succumbing to depression and anxiety.

Therefore select chew toys that are free from lead and cadmium. Dog toys that contain DEHP- bis (2-ethylhexl) phthalate have been found to have a huge effect on the reproductive system of rats, even at very low doses. Toy products from Cordura like the Frisbee contain no detectable amounts of lead, cadmium, or phthalates. Use non-toxic tennis balls from Planet Dog or other reputable sources. These balls are not only indestructible; they are entirely free of phthalates and heavy metals.

Non-toxic play toys are very important for all Vizsla puppies that experience stress when left alone. These toys serve as anxiety busters, and give your Vizsla puppy something to do when left alone.

Puppyhood does not last for very long, and is a very special time in everyone's lives. It is during the puppyhood stage that training, playing, socializing and all the preparation that you do with your Vizsla puppy needs to be taken seriously.

Puppies need so much more than love. They also need you to keep them safe and out of trouble. Vizsla pups can get themselves into plenty of trouble. Every single interaction that you will have with your Vizsla puppy will be firmly imprinted. Meet your puppy's emotional needs first, then learn how to live successfully with your Vizsla by training and protecting him.

9.) Summary for Puppy-Proofing Your Home

* Keep all of your cleaning products and dangerous chemicals stored securely in a cabinet where your puppy will not be able to access it.

* Store all food in the refrigerator or pantry where your puppy can't get it. Any food that you leave out needs to be in a tight-lidded container.

* Make sure that all of your medications and toiletries are stored in drawers or in your medicine cabinet.

* If you own a cat, make sure the litter box is stored somewhere your puppy can't get at it.

* Keep all electrical cords and loose blinds tied up so your puppy doesn't chew on or trip on the strings. Cover your outlets with outlet covers.

* Make sure you don't leave any small objects on the floor for your puppy to find. This includes things like childrens toys, small articles of clothing, jewelry, and more.

* Keep all doors closed to areas of the house that might be dangerous for your puppy (such as the garage or laundry room). You may even want to use baby gates to confine your puppy to whatever room you are in.

* Try not to use tobacco products in the house where your puppy might breathe the smoke. You should also dispose of ash and cigarette butts properly so your puppy doesn't get into them.

* If your yard does not already have a fence, consider having one installed so that your puppy can play outside safely.

* Keep all bodies of water (including sinks, bathtubs, toilets, etc.) covered. Even a small amount of water could pose a drowning risk for a small puppy.

* Keep a lid on all of your trash-cans and, if possible, keep them in a cabinet for an added level of security. You don't want your puppy to chew on something that he could choke on or that may be poisonous to him.

* Check to make sure that none of the plants in your house or on your property are toxic to dogs. If they are, make sure they are well out of your puppy's reach or put a fence around them.

In addition to following these steps to puppy-proof your home, you also need to carefully supervise your puppy when he is not in his crate. Your puppy doesn't know what is dangerous so it is your job to keep him safe.

10.) Where Will your Puppy Sleep

Deciding where your puppy will sleep is important. Many people choose to allow a dog on their bed, which is fine. However, it's important to understand separation anxiety if you sleep with your dog, and allow him to be with you at all times.

Separation anxiety is caused by over-attachment, and sleeping in your bed can be part of the reason for that. That's not to say that your puppy can't be allowed to sleep with you, just that you need to look carefully at the separation anxiety area of this book and decide how you will be safeguarding your own dog against it.

On the first night when you bring your puppy home I suggest that you don't leave him alone. Imagine how he would feel after being in the warmth of his nesting area with his mother and siblings to be then completely alone.

So make a conscious decision to stay in the room where your puppy will be sleeping for a couple of nights. You can also invest in a very specific puppy comforter meant for the first few nights in a new home, they can be warmed in the microwave and some even have heartbeats.

If your puppy is going to eventually be sleeping alone, then it's not a good idea to allow him to sleep on you. It would be much better to lie on the couch and have him on the ground beside you. That way you can offer a comforting hand when needed but he will be learning to leave behind the warmth of bodies at bedtime.

You can introduce the crate right at the beginning if you prefer, or wait until that first couple of nights are over. Eventually you will be able to leave a happily secure puppy in his sleeping place with ease.

An older dog that will be sleeping in another room in the beginning will probably howl and bark for the first few nights. Do not panic though because this is often due to unsettled feelings rather than severe separation anxiety. It usually wears off when the dog begins to feel secure.

11.) Setting Up Your Vizsla's Crate

The important thing about introducing your dog, whatever his age, to the crate is to make it a nice place that he finds welcoming. Put a cozy bed, toys and maybe even a stuffed Kong or other activity toy in the crate and allow your dog to sit in there with the door open to begin with.

If you need to have the crate close to you, in order to make your puppy feel secure, then this is fine too. But remember to then move it away later. The idea is to show your puppy that his crate is a most comfortable bedroom to the point that he chooses it as his resting place, all on his own.

When you do start to close the door, only do it for a short time. The idea is that your dog never thinks that he is going to be trapped against his will. Never just push the dog in and close the door as this can easily cause a phobia.

To make your Vizsla feel at home, place his crate somewhere permanent and place his food and water dishes nearby. You should also place a box with his toys in the area as well. Ideally, your Vizsla's crate should be kept in a location that is not in the middle of household activity but that is not too isolated either. You will be keeping your Vizsla in the crate overnight and when you are away from home during the house-training period, so place the crate somewhere that will not be in the way. If you do not like the idea of confining your Vizsla to the crate while you are away, you should set up a puppy play yard around the crate so your Vizsla has a little more space. He will still be confined but will be safe from potential hazards. He will be able to move around a little more to play with his toys.

12.) Bringing your Puppy/Adult Dog Home

Bringing a new dog home is an exciting and sometimes even a terribly scary time. If you follow the right stages of introduction for the dog though, both into your home and your family, everything should go smoothly.

During this area of the book I will talk about the first few days of a new dog being in your home. I will explain how he may be feeling, how you can communicate properly with your new dog and how to make life easy for all of you within this crucial settling in period.

One of the most tempting things to do when you bring a new dog home is celebrate their arrival. Everyone comes to meet the new family member and everyone wants a touch, particularly if the new arrival is a gorgeous Vizsla puppy.

When you bring a new puppy home it is important to remember that he will be confused and learning all of the time. That said, if the young dog has a lot of positive, gentle interaction even from day one it will be good for him and build his confidence. For this reason the new and young puppy may benefit from some careful visitors.

A new adult Vizsla is a different matter. An older dog will need a quiet time in the home for the first few days. The adult dog will not welcome a stream of visitors on day one.

The new dog will likely be scared and nervous. Remember that he will have little understanding about what is happening in his life and the best way you can approach this is keep quiet and allow him to get used to the new environment in his own time.

Similarly the dog should be left well alone by family members whilst he is settling in. He can get some positive attention and fuss if he asks for it, but should certainly not be cornered or forced to accept attention.

Many canine rescuers have to take dogs back into their care because a problem has occurred on day one or two that could easily have been avoided if the dog was given space and respect to settle into the new home before excited new owners forced their attentions on him.

A dog learns how to react to things, in his life, based upon past experiences. In addition, canine communication is very different to the communication that occurs between people. In actual fact the average new dog owner trying to make friends with a scared Vizsla by trying to touch him is having the exact opposite effect on their recently arrived dog.

I always ignore a new dog into the home. I barely look at them but offer attention if they ask for it. A very scared dog is allowed to hide where he is happy until he is ready to come out and learn to join in with everyday life in his own time.

Later on I will talk about body language and I think it is really important that you read through that, and the area on canine communication, before you bring your new dog home or at least as early as possible. By knowing how your dog acts when he feels a certain way you will be able to understand him better and start your new relationship off perfectly.

There is something that very few people tell you when they present you with a new dog, whatever age he may be. You may think that you have made a mistake.

This is an absolutely normal reaction to such a big change in your life. Whether you have brought home a scared teenage dog, a confident adult Vizsla or a needy puppy you may panic before things settle down.

With a puppy you will worry about why he is crying, whether you are feeding him properly, and how you can be sure that he stays happy and healthy.

When you bring home an adult dog, he may show separation anxiety, he may bark in the night for a few days and either be very clingy or completely aloof.

An adult dog may be so worried that he shows his teeth in the beginning. It's important not to crowd a new dog and everything will settle down quickly. The dog that is left to settle on his own will have no reason to feel threatened.

So all I can say to you is expect accidents, expect upheaval and expect things to change for a short time; then if the dog settles perfectly, far better than you expected, at least you were prepared

13.) First Introductions

When you introduce your new Vizsla to everyone else in the household it's important to be careful and respectful of how everyone feels and may react.

If you are bringing home a young puppy this will be easier because the puppy, when carefully handled, will generally be accepting of anyone and everyone. In the case of bringing a puppy home the other animals in the family must be considered.

Some older dogs that you may already have, are completely overwhelmed by the new squeaking, face licking, and over keen puppy.

In the beginning they may want to be nowhere near the baby dog. If you live with an older dog, ensure that he does not get walked on and harassed in those early days, particularly if he is worried. Similarly take extra care with the cat and any other pets you may have.

If you are bringing home an older dog, to a home with an existing dog, it is important to take all resources away that may cause friction. So pick up toys, treats and anything that either dog may guard. Remember that a new dog may feel insecure, therefore guard things for that reason alone.

It's a good idea to let two older dogs meet on neutral ground. At the park or somewhere similar rather than just bring the new dog directly home. Walking them together first will allow them to get used to the scent of each other and do the 'meet and greet' without the tension of perceived territory.

14.) Introducing Your Puppy to Children

Vizslas are a very social and people-oriented breed so they tend to get along well with children. This doesn't mean, however, that you can just put your puppy in a room with your kids and expect everything to be fine. Just as you need to ensure that your puppy is safe in your home, you also need to teach your kids how to properly handle the puppy for their own safety.

Introducing your children to the new dog is important. The kids must learn that the dog is not a toy and a young puppy is very fragile. Never leave your children alone with a new Vizsla of any age as this could be risky for all of them. Carefully explain to your children as much information as you can from this book and you will find that the dog and children become friends for life.

Just as you do between two dogs, watch out for resource guarding between dogs and children. Kids tend to grab at toys and food bowls, particularly the little ones. A dog could easily see this behavior as a threat and snap in return.

Similarly remember that any dog will not appreciate uncomfortable poking and prodding before he tells the child to go away, in the only way that he can.

Do not allow your child to follow a dog that has tried to move away from the attentions. This is a recipe for disaster because the dog can feel cornered and think he has to resort to aggression simply to be left alone.

If you manage your family well and teach an all-round respect you will be able to integrate the new dog in perfectly and before you know it, everyone will be great friends.

Follow the tips below to safely introduce your puppy to children:

1. Before you bring the puppy home, explain to your children how to properly handle the puppy. Tell them that the puppy is fragile and should be handled with care.

2. Tell your children to avoid over-stimulating the puppy. They need to be calm and quiet when handling him so he does not become frightened.

3. When it is time to make introductions, have your children sit on the floor in your home and bring the puppy to them.

4. Place the puppy on the floor near your children and let the puppy wander up to them when he is ready. Do not let your children grab the puppy.

5. Allow your children to calmly pet the puppy on his head and back when he approaches them. You may even give them a few small treats to offer the puppy.

Let your children pick up the puppy if they are old enough to handle him properly. If the puppy becomes fearful, have them put him back down.

If at any point during your introductions the puppy becomes afraid, you should take him out of the situation and place him in his crate where he can feel safe. Do not let your children scream or act too excited around the puppy until he gets used to them. It will take time for both your children and your puppy to get used to each other and you should supervise all interactions.

Please do remember, that where children are concerned or you already have a few pets, be extra careful of where your attentions go. After all, you want all of your pets to get along with each other, as well as your children. So do not create jealousy by fussing over your new Vizsla puppy and ignoring your other pets. Share your attention equally between all your pets, so that the relationship starts off well. Much of the future relationship between all of your pets, will depend on what happens during the first few days.

With children in the picture, it's important that this new relationship starts off well and gently. If your Vizsla puppy is your first puppy, as stated above, it's best to prepare young children with a firm explanation that all puppies need plenty of rest, quiet and gentleness. Prepare them ahead of time by showing them how to touch a small puppy, and what tone of voice to use i.e. low and comforting.

Children should never scream or run around a small, vulnerable puppy. They also should not pull his ears, tail or any other part of the puppy. It's best to be very firm about all the puppy rules ahead of time.

CHAPTER FOUR:

CARING FOR VIZSLA DOGS

Although you will have already covered aspects in this chapter in previous sections, we will go into a bit more detail here about certain necessary items. Caring for a Vizsla dog involves more than just feeding him and walking him. You also need to provide him with a safe and healthy environment in which to live. Vizslas are a very active breed so they need a certain amount of exercise as well as a lot of attention from their owners. In this chapter you will learn the basics about creating a healthy environment for your Vizsla at home including tips for setting up his crate area, other habitat requirements, and making sure that he gets enough exercise.

1.) Habitat Requirements for Vizslas

The Vizsla is a medium-sized breed so it does not require a great deal of space, but this breed will appreciate having room to run and play outdoors, if possible. One important thing to remember with this breed is that the Vizsla does not have a double-coat. He does not have an undercoat to protect him against harsh weather. This being the case, you should never keep your Vizsla outside for extended periods of time during the winter. On the opposite end of the spectrum, high temperatures can be dangerous for your dog as well. If you let your dog spend a lot of time in the yard during the winter, make sure that he has a shaded area to retreat to and plenty of fresh water at all times.

2.) Necessary Supplies and Equipment

Vizsla dogs do not need many accessories, but there are a few necessities you will want to have on hand.

Some of the necessary supplies and equipment for keeping Vizslas include the following:

* Food and water bowls
* Collar and leash
* Crate or kennel
* Blanket or dog bed
* Grooming supplies
* Assortment of toys

Food and Water Bowls – Your dog's food and water bowls do not necessarily need to be fancy, they just need to be sturdy and sanitary. The best material for food and water dishes is stainless steel because it is easy to clean and does not harbor bacteria. If you prefer, ceramic dishes are a good alternative and they come in a variety of colors to suit your preferences.

Collar and Leash – Having a high-quality collar and leash for your Vizsla is very important. It is also important that these items match your Vizsla's size. When your dog is a puppy you will need a small puppy collar that you can adjust as your puppy grows. Once your dog reaches his adult size you can get a slightly larger collar. The size of your dog's leash may change as he grows as well. When your puppy is young you will want a short leash to use for training and walks. Once your Vizsla grows up and gets some training you can upgrade to a longer leash.

Crate or Kennel – One of the most important accessories you need for your Vizsla is a crate or kennel. If you use it correctly your dog will not view time spent in the crate as punishment and there is no reason to believe that keeping your dog in a crate for short periods of time is cruel. If you use the crate properly while training your Vizsla he will come to view it as a place to call his own. It will become his place where he can go to take a nap or to get some time to himself if he wants it.

When selecting a crate for your Vizsla, size is very important. For the purpose of house training, you want to make sure that the crate is not too big. It should be just large enough for your puppy to stand, sit, lie down, and turn around comfortably. The key to crate training is to get your dog to think of the crate as his home, or his den. Dogs have a natural aversion to soiling their dens. If your puppy's crate is only large enough for him to sleep in, it will be more effective as a house-training tool. When your puppy grows up you can upgrade to a larger crate.

Blanket or Dog Bed – To make your dog's crate more comfortable, you should line it with a soft blanket or a plush dog bed. When you are house-training your Vizsla puppy, it is best to use an old blanket or a towel, just in case your puppy has an accident. Once your puppy is fully trained however, you can upgrade to a plush dog bed or a thicker blanket that will be more comfortable.

Grooming Supplies – Because the Vizsla has a very short coat you will not need to worry too much about shedding. You should still brush your dog's coat on at least a weekly basis in order to keep it in good health. You may also want to professionally groom your dog once or twice a year.

The grooming tools you may need to brush and bathe your Vizsla at home include:

* Dog nail clippers
* Gentle dog-friendly shampoo
* Shedding blade

The shedding blade will be your main grooming tool. You should use it three or four times a week to help remove dead hair from your dog's coat. The Vizsla has a very short coat but it sheds all year round so you should brush the coat regularly. You will find more detailed instructions for grooming your Vizsla in Chapter Seven of this book.

Assortment of Toys – As previously mentioned, offering your Vizsla an assortment of toys is very important. Having toys to play with will keep your dog occupied when you are unable to pay attention to him and it will also provide him with something to chew on instead of your furniture and other household items. Different dogs, like different toys, so your best bet is to buy several different kinds and let your dog choose which ones he likes best.

3.) Feeding Your Vizsla

Feeding your Vizsla a healthy diet is the key to maintaining his health and well-being. If you do not feed your Vizsla a high-quality food he could suffer from nutritional deficiencies as well as other health problems. Skimping on cheap dog food is false economy that could lead to health problems down the line and potentially expensive to treat. In this chapter you will learn the basics about dog nutrition and receive tips for feeding your Vizsla.

a.) Nutritional Requirements for Dogs

Just like all living things, dogs require a balance of nutrients in their diet to remain in good health. These nutrients include protein, carbohydrate, fats, vitamins, minerals, and water. Dogs are a carnivorous species by nature so meat plays an important role in their diet, but they do require some carbohydrates as well. Below you will find an overview of the nutritional needs for dogs in regard to each of the main nutrients. Keep these nutritional requirements in mind when selecting a dog food formula for your Vizsla.

Protein – This nutrient is composed of amino acids and it is essential for the growth and development of tissues, cells, organs, and enzymes in your dog's body. Protein can be obtained from both animal and plant-based sources, but animal-based proteins are the most biologically valuable for your dog. There are two categories of amino acids; essential and non-essential. Non-essential amino acids are those that your dog's body is capable of producing and essential amino acids are those he must get from his diet. The most important essential amino acids for a dog include lysine, arginine, phenylalanine, histidine, methionine, valine, leucine, threonine, and isoleucine.

Carbohydrate – The main role of carbohydrates in your dog's diet is to provide energy and dietary fiber. Dogs do not have a minimum carbohydrate requirement but they do need a certain amount of glucose to fuel essential organs like the brain. A dog's body is only capable of digesting certain kinds of carbohydrate and too much fiber in the diet is not good for them. The best types of fiber for a dog are moderately fermentable fibers such as beet pulp, cooked brown rice, and bran.

Fats – This is the most highly concentrated form of energy so it is an important part of your dog's diet. Fats provide your dog with twice the energy of protein and carbohydrates. Fats are also important for providing structure for cells and for producing certain types of hormones. They are also necessary to ensure that your dog's body can absorb fat-soluble vitamins. Your dog needs a balance of omega-3 and omega-6 fatty acids in his body and it is best if these fats come from animal-based sources instead of plant-based sources. Some of the best oils for dogs include salmon oil, general fish oil, cod liver oil, canola oil, and flaxseed oil.

Vitamins – Your dog's body is incapable of producing most vitamins, so it is essential that he get them through his diet. Some of the most important vitamins for dogs include vitamin A, vitamin D, vitamin E and vitamin C.

Minerals – Minerals are a type of inorganic compound that cannot by synthesized and thus must come from your dog's diet. The most important minerals for dogs include calcium, phosphorus, potassium, sodium, copper, zinc, and iron. Minerals are particularly important for developing and maintaining strong bones and teeth. Vitamins and minerals can be purchased and administered as a supplement with instruction from your veterinarian.

Water – Water is the most important nutrient for all animals. Your dog would be able to survive for a while without food if he had to, but he would only last a few days without water. Water accounts for as much as 70% of your dog's body-weight and even a 10% decrease in your dog's body water levels can be very dangerous. Provide your Vizsla with plenty of fresh water at all times.

B.) The Importance of Diet – Nutritional Deficiencies

Although we have covered diet in the feeding section, it is included here from a health, disease and deficiency point of view.

If you do not provide your dog with a healthy diet, his body will not be able to function as it should and he may become more likely to develop illnesses and infections. In addition to providing your dog with high-quality dog food, you also need to make sure that his diet provides certain nutrients. Dogs are prone to developing certain nutritional deficiencies which can produce some very real and dangerous symptoms.

Some of the nutritional deficiencies to which your Vizsla is most likely to be prone may include:

* General malnutrition
* Vitamin A deficiency
* Magnesium deficiency
* Iron deficiency anemia
* Vitamin E deficiency
* Calcium deficiency

General Malnutrition – Malnutrition is defined as the imbalanced, excessive, or insufficient consumption of nutrients. Some of the signs of malnutrition include an emaciated appearance, poor skin and coat quality, bad breath, swollen gums, abnormal stools, growth problems, poor immunity, lack of energy, and behavioral problems.

Vitamin A Deficiency – Vitamin A is a type of fat-soluble vitamin that comes from liver, dairy, and certain yellow vegetables. This vitamin is essential for the healthy formation of bones and teeth. It also plays a role in healthy skin, coat, and eyesight. A deficiency in Vitamin A may cause poor growth and development, skin problems, poor coat quality, eye problems, and immune problems.

Magnesium Deficiency – Magnesium and potassium are the most abundant substances in cells, so a magnesium deficiency can be very serious. Magnesium is required for most metabolic functions and in the development of healthy bones and tissue. Symptoms of magnesium deficiency include weakness, trembling, depression, behavioral changes, and loss of coordination. Careful treatment for this deficiency is essential because too much magnesium can be fatal for your dog.

Iron Deficiency Anemia – Iron is required to produce and develop red blood cells and those blood cells help to carry oxygen throughout your dog's body. A deficiency of iron can lead to anemia, a condition in which your dog doesn't have enough healthy red blood cells to carry oxygen to organs and muscles. Symptoms of iron deficiency anemia include loss of appetite, decreased growth, lethargy/weakness, depression, rapid breathing, and dark-colored stools.

Vitamin E Deficiency – Vitamin E is a fat-soluble vitamin that plays a role in metabolizing fats and supporting healthy cell function; it is also a type of antioxidant. Sources of vitamin E include liver, vegetable oil, wheat germ, and leafy green vegetables. A deficiency of vitamin E can lead to reproductive disorders as well as disorders of the liver, heart, muscle, nerves, and eyes. It can also have a negative impact on your dog's bowels.

Calcium Deficiency – Your dog requires a delicate balance of calcium and phosphorus to maintain healthy bones and teeth. Calcium is also important for nerve, heart and muscle function as well as blood clotting. A calcium deficiency can lead to spasms, lameness, heart palpitations, anxiety, bone fractures, arthritis, high blood pressure, and more. This type of deficiency is often caused by a high-meat diet because meat is very high in phosphorus – this can lead to an imbalance of phosphorus and calcium.

In addition to deficiencies in certain vitamins or minerals, dogs can also suffer from an excess of certain nutrients. For example, too much vitamin A can cause your Vizsla's bones to become brittle and his skin to become dry. An excess of vitamin D could cause your dog's bones to become too dense and for his tissue and joints to calcify. Too much vitamin C can lead to kidney stones, excess calcium can lead to phosphorus imbalances, and too much polyunsaturated fat (such as from fish oil) may lead to a vitamin E imbalance.

c.) Calorie Requirements for Dogs

Your dog requires a certain number of calories each day in order for his body to maintain proper function. Calorie needs for dogs vary from one breed to another and they also depend on the dog's age, size, sex, and activity level.

On the next page you will find a chart outlining the basic calorie needs for dogs at different ages:

The calorie information in the chart is a basic guideline. Your dog's individual needs may be different. The best way to determine how many calories your Vizsla actually needs is to calculate his Resting Energy Requirement (RER) and to then modify it according to his age and activity level. The formula for calculating your dog's RER is as follows:

RER = 30 x (weight in kg) + 70

For example, if your Vizsla weighed 45 pounds, you would use the following formula: RER = 30 x (45/2.205) +70. So

Calorie Needs For Dogs (Per Day)

Type of Dog	*10 Lbs*	*15 Lbs*	*20 Lbs*
Puppy (Under 4 Months)	*618 Calories*	-	-
Puppy (Over 4 Months)	*412 Calories*	-	-
Normal Adult Dog	*329 Calories*	*438 Calories*	*547 Calories*
Active Adult Dog	*412 Calories*	*548 Calories*	*684 Calories*
Pregnant Female	*618 Calories*	*822 Calories*	*1,026 Calories*
Lactating Female	*824+ Calories*	*1,096+ Calories*	*1,368+ Calories*

(45/2.205) = 20.40816327, then multiply that by 30 = 612.244898, then add 70 = 682 rounded down to the nearest whole number. You will note that in order to determine your dog's weight in kilograms you need to divide it by 2.205 first. So using our formula and the example given as shown above, a 45-pound Vizsla has an estimated RER of about 682 calories. To determine your dog's daily energy requirements you will need to multiply his RER by a factor that varies by age and activity level. Use the chart on the next page to determine what number to multiply your dog's RER by: (The RER chart is shown on the next page)

So following on, if we use another example, in this case our 20 Lb. dog in the chart, to get to 684 we calculate as follows:

20 divided by 2.205 = 9.070295.
9.070295 x 30 = 272.1088.
272.1088 + 70 = 342.1088

Now taking into consideration the activity level of the dog as light so multiply the RER by 2; we multiply 342.1088 by 2 = 684 rounded to the nearest whole number

Based on the information in the chart above, you can see that puppies and pregnant dogs have much higher calorie needs than adult dogs. When your Vizsla puppy is growing he will need to eat a lot more than he will when he is fully grown. Puppy foods are typically higher in both protein and calories than adult dog foods. This accounts

Resting Energy Requirements (RER)

Type of Dog	*Daily Calorie needs*
Weight Loss	*1.0 x RER*
Normal Adult (Neutered)	*1.6 x RER*
Normal Adult (Intact)	*1.8 x RER*
Lightly Active Adult	*2.0 x RER*
Moderately Active Adult	*3.0 x RER*
Pregnant (First 42 Days)	*1.8 x RER*
Pregnant (Last 21 Days)	*3.0 x RER*
Lactating Female	*4.8 x RER*
Puppy (2 to 4 Months)	*3.0 x RER*
Puppy (4 to 12 Months)	*2.0 x RER*

for the needs of growing puppies. In pregnant females you typically do not need to start increasing rations until the last three weeks of gestation. Once the dog gives birth, her calorie needs will increase again so that she can produce enough milk for her puppies. The more puppies in the litter, the higher her calorie needs will be.

When your dog gets older, his calorie needs will drop. Senior dogs typically require 20% fewer calories than younger dogs because their metabolisms slow down and they become less active. Many dogs become overweight as they age because their owners do not reduce their feeding portions to account for changes in metabolism and energy. Once a dog becomes obese it can be difficult for him to lose weight, so be especially careful with your dog's diet once he reaches "senior" level around 7 years of age.

So what is a good diet choice for your Vizsla dog Well you have many options and can even mix and match, as I do, to keep things interesting for your dog.

Once again, the preceding is intended to give you a rough idea of the amount of food your dog is likely to need per day, depending on his circumstances. In our case, a Vizsla is an active dog and will therefore have greater food needs than a less active dog.

D.) How to Choose a Healthy Dog Food

Now that you have a basic understanding of your dog's nutritional needs you are ready to learn how to choose a healthy dog food. If you walk down the aisles at your local pet store you could easily be overwhelmed by the sheer number of options you have.

Not only are there many different brands to choose from but most brands offer several different flavors or formulas. In this section you will learn the basics about how to determine whether a commercial dog food is healthy or not.

Commercial Dog Food

Do not rule out a great quality dried food, mixed with wet food of something similar. When you are choosing a commercial food though keep in mind that less is more, don't look at the promises on the packaging but turn it around and look at the ingredients on the back, this will tell you so much more.

If there is anything that you don't recognize don't buy the food until you have found out what the ingredient is. If the main ingredient is some kind of meat followed by the words "meal' of 'derivatives' don't buy the food.

Get Cooking

Your second option is to cook your dog's food at home. This is actually quite easy and there is no reason why you can't alternate between home prepared dog food and a good quality commercial food. Variety is the spice of life after all and this applies to dogs too.

A careful mix of sweet potatoes, green leafy veggies, beans and legumes with added white fish or other protein source is a perfect home-made dog's dinner. You can add some soy cream or cheese for taste but not dairy food as it's not generally suitable for adult animals. Adding some type of oil is also good for the coat and the joints and you can alternate with oil type, flax and fish oils are good for the heart whilst vegetable oils are good for the skin and coat.

If you make a big pot of food at a time and vary the types of carbohydrate and protein then you should easily meet all of your dog's vitamin and mineral needs over a few weeks recurring.

If you want to be extra sure that you are meeting your dog's nutritional needs then alternate between commercial food and home-made then add a digestive enzyme with vitamin supplement prepared for your dog. This type of supplement is available widely in pet stores. Having said that, be careful not to give your dog vitamin and mineral supplements for the sake of it. Many good quality commercial mixes contain a correct balance of vitamins and minerals. As noted previously, too much vitamins and minerals can have as adverse an effect as too little. If you are in any doubt, feed a correctly balance commercial feed and follow their recommendations. Once you get a better understanding of alternative feeds, then you can mix and match.

Raw Feeding

Over the last few years raw feeding has become increasingly popular and most that try it never go back to cooked food for their pets. Raw feeding is so popular that manufacturers are preparing raw food in the same way as they have been, for years, with cooked dog food.

The idea behind this feeding type is that the dog's diet is as natural as possible. It is based upon the diet a wild carnivore would eat. Some meat and offal, some bones and green vegetables; all raw, are fed to the dog in order to mirror the wild diet. The wild diet would usually have been small prey animals, grass, greens and bones.

Advocates of this feeding type usually state that it is the best decision that they have ever made on behalf of their dog whilst there are very few that turn away from raw feeding after trial-ing it.

There are some precautions to be aware of if you are considering raw feeding though. There have been some links between infection of arthritic joints and raw meat. Similarly too many raw bones can cause digestive blockages, and bones in general can be terribly dangerous for a dog. Some experts also believe that our dogs were more scavengers as they developed and ate less meat than we think.

I suggest that if this feeding type is something you may consider then do a lot of research first. The commercial raw foods are varying in quality much like the commercial cooked dog foods. If you are putting your dog's diet together at home then it's vital to consider varied and balanced nutrition.

If you are changing your dog's food at all then remember to wean gradually from one to the other as a quick change can easily be the cause of stomach upsets.

E.) Types of Commercial Dog Food

There are three main types of commercial dog food – wet, dry, and semi-moist. Dry dog foods are the most commonly used and they are also referred to as "kibble". This type of food is typically packed in a bag and they are usually extruded in the form of pellets. Dry dog foods come in a wide variety of flavors and formulas and they have a fairly low moisture content. Wet dog food obviously has a higher moisture content. They are typically cooked at very high temperatures to sterilize them and then packaged in pressure-sealed containers. Semi-moist dog foods come in the form of soft, chewy pellets typically packaged in pouches or sachets.

In addition to these types of commercial dog food there are a few other options. Dehydrated dog food is becoming popular among pet owners who want to feed their dogs fresh or raw food but who want a product with a longer shelf life. Fresh dog food comes in refrigerated or frozen varieties and it is one of the most expensive options when it comes to commercial dog food. Fresh dog food can also be freeze-dried to remove most of the moisture content (thereby increasing the shelf life) without resulting in a loss of nutrients by cooking.

The type of dog food you choose for your Vizsla is largely a matter of preference. Most dog owners choose dry food because it is the most cost-effective option and because it lasts the longest. If your dog has food allergies or special dietary restrictions, a fresh or frozen dog food may be a better option because these foods are often made with limited ingredients. Senior dogs, who have trouble chewing dry food may prefer moist or semi-moist foods. You can also just soak dry food in water or broth to soften it.

F.) Reading the Ingredients List

Once you've decided what type of commercial food you prefer you can start to evaluate different brands and formulas. The best way to do this is by looking at the label and the ingredients list. When you evaluate a bag of dog food, the first thing you should look for is a statement of nutritional adequacy from the American Association of Feed Control Officials (AAFCO).

The statement should look something like this:

"[Product Name] is formulated to meet the nutritional levels established by the AAFCO Dog Food nutrient profiles for [Life Stage]."

The American Association of Feed Control Officials is responsible for monitoring and regulating what goes into animal feed including pet foods. This organization has set standards that pet foods must meet in order to be considered nutritionally adequate for dogs in certain life stages; puppy, adult, and senior. If the dog food label does not carry an AAFCO statement of nutritional adequacy, you should move on to another option. On the other hand, just because a product carries the AAFCO statement doesn't necessarily mean that it is good for your dog.

In the United Kingdom, the Pet Food Manufacturer's Association (PFMA) exists to provide pet owners with guidance for selecting pet foods. This organization is the principal trade body for the U.K. pet food industry with more than 70 member companies, representing about 90% of the U.K. pet food market. The PFMA does not put a statement on pet food labels like AAFCO; but they do strive to raise pet food industry standards and to promote pet food products deemed as safe and nutritious.

For more information about pet food labeling standards in the U.K., visit the PFMA website here:

http://www.pfma.org.uk/labelling

The best way to truly evaluate the nutritional value of a pet food is to examine the ingredients list. Dog food labels include a complete list of ingredients that is organized in descending order by volume. This means that the ingredients present in the highest quantity/volume appear at the beginning of the list. This makes it easy for you to get a quick sense of a product's nutritional value. If the first few ingredients are healthy ingredients, the product might be a good choice. If however, the first few ingredients are low-quality fillers, you should move on.

When evaluating the ingredients list for a commercial dog food, you want to see a high-quality source of protein listed first. Fresh meats like chicken, turkey, beef, and fish are good options but do not be turned off if you see something like chicken meal. Fresh meats contain about 80% water so, once the dog food is cooked, their weight is much less than the original. Meat meals have already been cooked down to a moisture content around 10% so they contain up to 300% more protein than fresh meats. A high-quality commercial dog food might list a fresh meat first followed by a meat meal second.

In addition to high-quality protein sources, you should also look for digestible carbohydrates and animal-based fats in the ingredients list. Carbohydrates that are easily digestible for dogs include things like cooked brown rice, oats, and barley. Be wary of wheat and corn-based products however, because these ingredients often trigger food allergies in dogs and they are low in nutritional value. The number of carbohydrate sources on the ingredients list is also important to consider. Dogs do not require a great deal of carbohydrate. Only about 15% of your dog's diet should come from carbohydrates. Low-quality dog foods contain as much as 30% to 70% of this nutrient.

If you see an ingredient like chicken fat or poultry fat on the label for a commercial pet food, do not be turned off as it is a good thing! As you learned previously, fats are a highly concentrated form of energy and they play an important role in your dog's diet. Fats from animal-based sources are particularly beneficial so you should look for things like chicken fat and fish oil in your dog's food. Plant-based fats like flaxseed oil and canola oil can also be beneficial but animal-based fats are more biologically valuable to your dog.

In addition to the main ingredients on a dog food label you also need to pay attention to the things near the end of the list. This is where pet food manufacturers like to sneak in things like artificial flavors, colorants, and preservatives. Avoid ingredients with the word "by-product" attached, as well as chemical preservatives like BHA and BHT. Be aware that these ingredients might be spelt out instead of abbreviated. You should also avoid things like corn syrup, MSG, food dyes, and low-quality filler ingredients like corn and wheat gluten.

G.) Vizsla Feeding – What's in the Tin

The quality of commercially prepared dog food is a hot topic. The dog food industry is a high earning one and often owned by huge corporations that often put profit before the health of our dogs.

Many dog food ingredients are not fit for human consumption and although vitamins are added to dog foods we cannot be certain whether they are of good enough quality to have an effect on the health of our dogs.

Unless an ingredients list on a bag or tin of dog food is completely transparent, the meat within dog food is usually rendered and described as 'meal' or 'derivatives'.

But what do these hazy terms actually mean?

Rendering is a process which involves putting bones, carcasses, beaks, hooves and tails into a huge tub and heating it so high that any virus cells, bacteria or antibiotic content dies. The fat content rises to the top and is scooped away.

The remnants are ground up into a hot pink sludge of body parts. And this substance is what will eventually become commercial dog food. Does it sound terrifying? It does, that's because it is. Rendered foods are permanently deemed unfit for human consumption for health reasons. Yet we unknowingly feed it to our dogs.

After the food becomes kibble it is colored to look nice and then sprayed with the aforementioned fat, in order to tempt dogs to eat it.

Tinned foods have a lot of salt added, as do the little pouches meant for small dogs, which is no good for the dog's heart.

Thankfully and due to many different investigations inclusive of the dog food project by Sabine Contreras many smaller businesses are developing better food, made from whole food ingredients that are much better for our dogs. ***www.dogfoodproject.com*** describes the entire investigation and is well worth a read.

H.) Commercial Foods for Vizslas

The commercial dog foods available in your area might differ according to the pet store chains available as well as the distribution policies for certain brands.

Below you will find a list of several commercial dog food formulas that are intended for active breeds like the Vizsla:

Nutro Natural Choice – High Endurance Adult Dog Food

This commercial dry food formula is specially designed for physically active dogs, made with a 30/20 protein-to-fat ratio for optimal energy levels and improved muscle recovery. This formula lists chicken meal, whole brown rice, rice bran, chicken fat, and whole grain oatmeal as the top five ingredients. The fact that chicken meal is listed first means that this formula is very high in protein. Meat meals have already been cooked down to a low moisture level which means that they are a much more highly concentrated source of protein than fresh meats. Whole brown rice and whole grain oatmeal are both complex carbohydrates and good sources of dietary fiber for dogs. Chicken fat is also a good ingredient because it provides your dog with essential fatty acids.

Breeder's Choice Active Care Healthy Joint Dog Food

This dry food formula from Breeder's Choice includes brown rice, chicken meal, chicken cartilage, chicken fat, and flaxseed as the top five ingredients. It would be better if the chicken meal, were listed first and the brown rice second, but this formula is still a good source of protein and digestible carbohydrates. Both the chicken fat and flaxseed provide essential fatty acids. In fact, flaxseed is the richest plant source of omega-3 fatty acids. Overall, this product provides balanced nutrition for your Vizsla.

Earthborn Holistic Primitive Natural Dry Dog Food

This dry dog food formula from Earthborn is made with several high-quality sources of protein including turkey meal, chicken meal, and whitefish meal. It is also made with chicken fat for fatty acids and potatoes for gluten-free carbohydrates. Another valuable inclusion in this dry food formula is an assortment of chelated minerals. Chelated minerals are found in high-quality dog foods and they consist of minerals that have been chemically bonded to protein molecules which makes them more readily available for your dog's body to absorb.

Performatrin Ultra Grain-Free Dry Dog Food

Performatrin Ultra dry dog food offers healthy, balanced nutrition for your Vizsla and it has the bonus of being completely grain-free. The top five ingredients for this dry food formula are de-boned turkey, turkey meal, peas, salmon meal and duck meal. The fact that high-quality sources of protein are listed four times within the top five ingredients speaks of the high protein content of this formula. It is also worth noting that a number of fresh vegetables are included for dietary fiber as well as various vitamins and minerals. This formula also includes chelated minerals and probiotics to facilitate healthy digestion.

I.) How Much to Feed Your Vizsla

As you have already learned, your Vizsla's calorie needs will vary according to his age and activity level. When your Vizsla is a puppy it is recommended that you allow him to eat as much as he likes. Most dogs are good about eating when they are hungry and stopping when they are full. Keeping your puppy's food dish full will ensure that he gets the calories he needs to fuel his growth and development.

Once your puppy reaches maturity you should start rationing his meals. You can choose how many meals to give your Vizsla each day, but most dog owners recommend dividing your dog's daily portion into two meals. To help you determine how much to feed your dog, follow the feeding suggestions on the dog food package. Keep in mind that feeding suggestions are just that, suggestions, so you may need to make adjustments. Start off with the recommended amount for a few weeks. If your dog gains weight you'll need to cut back a bit. If he loses weight, you should increase his rations a bit. You can always ask your veterinarian for suggestions if you aren't sure whether your dog is at a healthy weight.

Another factor you need to consider in regard to feeding your Vizsla is how many treats you give him. When you are training your puppy, you should use very small treats. Even if your puppy eats a lot of them, however, it will not be a problem because he needs a lot of calories to fuel his growth. Once your Vizsla is fully mature, however, you should limit the number of treats you give him to avoid going over his daily calorie allotment.

J.) Toxic Foods Affecting Vizsla Dogs

In addition to making sure that you provide your Vizsla with a healthy diet, you also need to be careful NOT to feed him certain foods. It can be tempting to give your dog a few scraps from your plate but certain "people" foods can actually be toxic for your dog.

If your Vizsla gets into a food that he shouldn't have, you should call the Pet Poison Control Hotline. The specialist on the other end of the line will be able to tell you if the amount your dog ingested is potentially toxic. If it is, they will walk you through the steps to induce vomiting to purge the item from your dog's stomach, or recommend that you take your dog to an emergency vet. You may also be able to speak to a licensed veterinarian on the phone for a fee around $65 (£42.25).

<u>Below you will find a list of foods that can be harmful to your Vizsla:</u>

* Alcohol
* Apple seeds
* Avocado
* Cherry pits
* Chocolate
* Cocoa mulch fertilizer
* Coffee
* Garlic
* Grapes/raisins
* Gum (can cause blockages and sugar free gums may contain the toxic sweetener Xylitol)
* Hops
* Macadamia nuts
* Mold
* Mushrooms
* Mustard seeds
* Nuts
* Onions and onion powder/ leeks
* Peach pits

* Potato leaves/stems
* Rhubarb leaves
* Tea
* Tomato leaves/stems
* Walnuts
* Xylitol
* Yeast dough

K.) Toxic Plants Affecting Vizsla Dogs

Not only do you need to be careful about which foods you keep out of your Vizsla's reach, there are also plants that can be toxic to all dogs. If you have any of the houseplants listed below in your house, make sure to keep them well out of your dog's reach. For toxic outdoor plants, remove them from your property or fence them off for your dog's safety.

A list of toxic plants for dogs can be found below:

* Azalea
* Baneberry
* Bird-of-paradise
* Black locust
* Buckeye
* Buttercup
* Caladium
* Castor bean
* Chock-cherries
* Christmas rose
* Common privet
* Cowslip
* Daffodil
* Day lily
* Delphinium
* Easter lily
* Elderberry
* Elephant's ear
* English Ivy
* Foxglove
* Holly
* Horse-chestnut
* Hyacinth
* Iris
* Jack-in-the-pulpit
* Jimsonweed
* Laurels
* Lily of the valley
* Lupines

* May-apple
* Mistletoe
* Morning glory
* Mustards
* Narcissus
* Nightshade
* Oaks
* Oleander
* Philodendron
* Poinsettia
* Poison hemlock
* Potato
* Rhododendron
* Rhubarb
* Sago palm
* Sorghum
* Wild black cherry
* Wild radish
* Wisteria
* Yew

Chapter Five:

Early Training

Every time I learn something new about the biology of dogs I realize how important puppy learning is. Those early stages not only build the body of your Vizsla dog, but also his mind. Which is exactly why I wanted to share these stages of puppy learning with you now.

1.) The Stages of Puppy Learning

Dogs are, with no shadow of doubt, a mixture of their genetic influence and their prior learning. Learning and experiences go right back to conception too, shaping the puppy whilst he is still in the womb.

The influence on a puppy will begin with the hormones in his mother's body during her pregnancy, and end the day that the puppy dies an old and wise dog.

A stressed and insecure mother dog will be producing hormones such as cortisol and adrenaline whilst her puppies are developing in her womb.

Excess stress related hormones released during development has already been shown to change a puppy's behavior, usually later as he grows into an adult dog.

Even with the most careful socialization schedule, a poor gestation period can lead to a less emotionally stable dog; another reason not to buy a puppy from a pet store or puppy farm.

So how does a carefully bred puppy develop when he has a happy and, well cared for and stable mom

a.) Your Neonatal Puppy!

When the mother dog is stable and healthy, she will usually give birth to healthy puppies. At the beginning, up until twelve to fourteen days old the puppies are in a stage of development called the Neonatal stage.

Their eyes are still closed and they are completely helpless, simply feeding and sleeping. At this point the puppy brain is not fully developed and many of the neurons still have some growing to do.

The puppy from birth does have a heat seeking nose and uses it to find the warmth of his mother if separated from her. The puppies are also stimulated to toilet at this point, by their mother's licking.

Tests have shown that puppies who are handled carefully for a few minutes a day, at this point, develop into dogs more able to cope with the world later on. This should obviously be carried out in the vicinity of the Mother dog and certainly cause her no stress.

Many professional dog training establishments utilize this knowledge now and carefully handle puppies from birth.

b.) A Puppy in Transition

After the neonatal stage the puppies begin to learn about the world. This stage of development is called the transition period. This is a busy period for learning and change which lasts until the puppy is around twenty days old.

During this period the dog's eyes open, his ear canals form and he starts to use his senses. The puppy begins social learning and begins to bond with his siblings and mother, he will also protest if moved away from the litter. The puppy begins to learn appeasement behavior, such as tail wagging and muzzle licking along with other forms of canine communication.

Again, the puppy will develop into a more confident older dog if he is carefully and kindly introduced to a variation of things during this phase. Toys, floor surfaces, noises and gentle handling all aid social confidence later on.

C.) The Socialization Stage

Socialization time lasts from the end of the transition period right through to the twelve week old point. This is crucial learning time that cannot be completely changed later on.

The dog's behavior is shaped by this learning period and therefore this should be filled with positive social experiences that will shape a happy and confident puppy and older .

A good breeder will ensure that the puppies in their care have as much positive social contact as possible. The new dog owner of an eight week old puppy will need to continue this careful social learning into adulthood.

The dog that misses out on proper social learning will struggle for the rest of his or her life. The Vizsla dog that is poorly socialized will probably, eventually bark to warn away everything that is deemed scary. The poorly socialized dog may feel that he has to show defensive aggression.

Although behavior modification can be carried out, a dog that has not been properly raised and socialized can never be truly 'fixed'. The owner will simply need to learn to modify the behavior if possible, and manage it if not.

2.) Vizsla Toilet Training

Do you remember the old saying 'rub his nose in it' For many years this was how house-training was carried out. Poor dogs. In this area of the book we are going to talk about puppy toilet training the right way.

Housebreaking a Vizsla dog need not be a difficult task. It is simply a case of teaching your dog, as soon as you can, that outside is where the toileting happens.

Vizsla toilet training for success is a matter of putting everything that you can into that first few days. The more times your puppy gets it right in the beginning the quicker he will learn what you want from him.

A.) What Will You Need

For perfect Vizsla toilet training you won't really need a great deal. Some puppy pads or newspaper, an odor neutralizer and a sharp eye along with a swift movement if you notice your puppy needs to go.

I say an odor neutralizer because a generic cleaning product is not enough. General cleansing fluid does not rid the environment of the smell and the dog will always return to a smell when looking for a toilet area. Odor neutralizers literally take the urine into their own particles then disperse and destroy it.

B.) Good Toilet Training Practice

Get into your mind, the idea that for the next few days, you will be a puppy taxi. This involves ferrying your dog outside at least every hour to two hours. In addition, in the case of accidents, picking your little dog up and relocating him to the right place as he starts to toilet.

Similarly it is a good idea to expect to use puppy pads or newspapers in the beginning.

The idea is that in an ideal world, the puppy will go outside to toilet every time. It is still a good idea to have pads present though just in case you miss an opportunity to get him out. The puppy pads can be phased out later but your puppy has a tiny bladder at the moment and the puppy pad can help with any unexpected toilet mishaps.

You can gradually move the puppy pad toward the external door as the puppy becomes familiar with how to use them. Eventually when the dog heads for it, you can get him straight out of the back door.

Then in time, you may only need to put puppy pads down overnight until your dog's bladder and bowel matures.

Dog understanding begins with knowing that a dog of any age will repeat any behavior which is rewarded. Things get a little complicated when you look further into it but generally this is the baseline truth.

In addition, the act of rewarding something also teaches the dog to repeat it enough times for it to become a habit.

Putting this into practice, particularly where toilet training is concerned, is actually quite an easy – three step process as follows;

Step One

* Get the environment ready for toilet training by working out where the puppy will be expected to toilet outdoors and sorting out your puppy pads for indoors.

* Place your puppy pads nearby indoors. Puppy pads can be used as the indoor toilet for now whilst your puppy is learning and through the night. As mentioned before, you can substitute pads for newspaper.

* Commit yourself to look carefully at your puppy for signs that he may need to go, he may lick his lips, yawn or glance at you. Or if you notice him wandering about, sniffing or circling, anticipate he may need to toilet. If you notice him about to go, it may also be an idea to say something like 'outside for toilets', or 'outside for a wee wee'. You will hopefully get to the stage where as soon as he hears this, he knows you want him to do his toileting outside and will wait at the door. Most dogs get to the stage where they bark to let you know they want letting out to do their toilet business.

Step Two

* Take your puppy outdoors every hour at least. Take him out after he has eaten, slept, played and had a drink because these are the times he will most likely need to go. Take him and wait with him until your puppy toilets, if he needs to.

* Remember this is a baby in the big wild world and he is probably quite

insecure. If you push any puppy outdoors to toilet, then leave him out there alone, you are teaching him something and it's not good toilet training.

* So wait with your puppy until he has indeed done his business or he may just come inside and pee at your feet.

* Taxi your puppy outside or to the pad at this point if he has an accident. If he toilets on the pad of his own accord then praise him, as this is a step closer to toileting outside and a step further away from doing it on the floor in the house. You can also begin to move the pad away gradually towards the external door.

Step Three

* When your puppy 'goes' in the place you want him to, it is vital to reward the behavior. Remember that he won't know what you want from him unless you show/tell him. A carefully rewarded behavior will always be repeated.

* Watch your puppy for accidents. Any signs that he may need to toilet, then scoop him up to take him outside or to the nearest puppy pad. This is where you employ that puppy taxi habit.

* Even if your dog has begun to go in the wrong place quickly and quietly ferry him along to his legitimate toileting area. This way you will be alleviating any confusion that he may have about the location of his toilet area.

* Even if he does a tiny bit in the right area still reward him. It can be difficult to learn this for a puppy, particularly as his brain and bladder are still developing; so be kind and patient.

* Keep your eyes peeled because the more successes at this point, the quicker your Vizsla puppy will become housebroken.

C.) No Punishment

If your puppy has an accident then you were either not watching him carefully enough or you have not taken him out enough. Don't punish accidents. Simply clean up, and tell yourself that you will do better next time.

Punishment of accidents will cause anxiety around toileting for your puppy and this will simply lead to more accidents. Punishment may even lead to the puppy feeling he needs to eat his own poop, that's not a fair way to raise a puppy.

Older dogs can have housebreaking problems based on a few different things. If a dog has never lived indoors or been house-trained, then he may toilet indoors. This is not his fault as he hasn't been taught the social etiquettes that we live by. You should therefore apply the steps above in the same way to show the dog what you want.

When you bring a rescued Vizsla home, it's important to expect at least a couple of accidents, because he or she will be confused and nervous.

d.) Scent Marking

Male dogs may scent mark in the new home if they are un-neutered or particularly nervous.

Scent marking is the dog's way of showing other dogs that he is there, and can be a nervous reaction or a hormonal response.

Castration can help with the male dog that scent marks, but is not a definite solution as it can cause further insecurity in some worried dogs. It is worth speaking to your vet if you are having a problem like this.

e.) Elderly Dogs

Dogs can lose control of their bladder with old age. This is a sad situation and one which we have to adapt to because we love our dogs.

The vet can prescribe specific treatment for leaking and may need to check out your dog's overall health if this is an issue.

Many dogs fail to make it through the night in the last months/years without needing to go out.

Again, the best solution is to put down plenty of newspaper for him to go on. Cleaning this up in the morning is a small sacrifice to pay, as you need to make things as easy and comfortable for them as possible.

3.) Why Socialize

We have dealt with the importance of socialization earlier, but go into it a bit more detailed here. Socialization is a complete topic in itself. There are so many dogs in rescue shelters and homes that simply do not know how to react in social situations.

This is because they have never learned what to do in the company of other dogs, children and crowded areas or around other animals.

Stop for a moment and think of street dogs in Europe and similar places. You never see them fighting do you? They manage to get on with no tension and certainly no aggression. They never bark at cars or people.

The street dogs never seem to worry too much about their surroundings. Which points to the fact that there must be a specific reason for the behavior. You guessed it, the reason for poorly socialized dogs is us humans.

We leash them up, stop them interacting, panic when another dog comes towards them and often keep them well away from social situations altogether. Then when a puppy gets to a few months old we complain about their social behavior.

As mentioned previously, it is possible to grasp back some social skills with an older dog, after the socialization boat has sailed. Yet the dog that isn't positively socialized as a puppy, will never really be completely relaxed in new circumstances.

Positive socialization should incorporate everything that you possibly can into a dog's everyday life as early as possible. Not only that though, every experience should be positive.

A good socialization schedule will include positive experiences of and with:

Important!

* As many dogs as possible
* Buses
* Cars
* Children
* Domestic animals
* Farmed animals
* People of all ages
* Push-chairs
* Sounds such as recorded thunder and fireworks
* The groomer (if you are to use a professional)
* The veterinary surgery
* Trains or trams
* Unusual looking people (those wearing hats and unusual clothing)
* Wildlife

Your dog will need to learn canine manners from other dogs and is socialized with all of the other things to build his personal confidence and ability to cope in new situations as he grows.

Lack of social skills in the Vizsla can easily become borderline aggressive behavior because of his tenacious genetic need to defend himself.

So introduce him to as many social situations as possible. He can then learn that most situations are nothing to be afraid of. When you do encounter any of the above, as with any training, always give him lots of praise and show him how pleasant these encounters can be.

4.) OTHER TRAINING CONSIDERATIONS

A.) AVOID OVER ATTACHMENT

When your puppy is feeling secure, it is vital to teach him that alone time is normal, even if your lifestyle dictates that the dog will never be left alone, because this prepares your dog for life. Remember the Vizsla can live to a ripe old age and even beyond, so who knows what the future holds

Later on we will talk about separation anxiety and how it develops. Yet if you start leaving your puppy early in his life you can certainly minimize the risk. So set up times where you leave him for a short time and try not to allow your puppy to trail around the house after you, following you into every room.

The idea is not to allow your puppy to develop over attachment to you. When a dog becomes over attached they cannot cope with being left alone, simply because you are not there.

Practice leaving your dog with a stuffed Kong, the radio or television on and pop out for a few minutes every day after the first few days.

Make this a priority and part of your dog's learning program because by doing this you minimize the risk of your Vizsla puppy developing distressing separation anxiety later on.

B.)Puppy Classes and Playtime!

Puppy classes can be so important to a young dog's social development that many veterinary surgeries offer them for free to new clients.

It is very easy to take a dog away from the litter and for the next few weeks only provide him with human contact. Particularly because vaccinations are given around the crucial socialization period and dog owners are advised to keep their puppy away from risky areas that may harbor disease.

The worrying thing with this, is that the time between leaving the litter and twelve weeks old is the crucial learning stage where social skills and canine manners are developed. No matter what we do, or how hard we try, we simply cannot replace another dog's place for the puppy who is learning social skills.

Puppy classes provide essential canine contact, play and sometimes even education for the developing puppy. Every Vizsla dog should either attend a puppy class or get together with as many other dogs as possible, as he grows, in order to prevent fear and anxiety later in life.

C.) A Nice Relaxed Walk

Taking your Vizsla for a walk can be a wonderful experience or quite stressful all round. It is actually a lot easier to improve behavior on the leash than you may think though.

Walking Equipment

Dog walking equipment should be introduced carefully, particularly to a puppy, and only the kindest collars or harness types should be used.

The harness is generally better than a collar, as it redistributes the weight of his body and naturally, immediately stops him pulling on the leash.

Dogs are far easier to control on walks when wearing a harness and there is no nasty pulling and coughing, as often happens on a standard collar and leash.

There is never a need to use choke or metal collars on dogs. The same result is easily achievable by using humane equipment and the smallest amount of positive training.

When you first introduce a Vizsla puppy, or older dog, to a collar or harness make it a nice and positive event. Pop it onto the dog and play for a while, then remove it again whilst the dog is still happy.

After doing this a few times, add the leash and allow the dog to trail it behind in the house or garden. Then your puppy should be sufficiently used to it and will be ready to go for a walk.

The following training steps are to help you prevent pulling on the leash. They are simply to make your Vizsla walking experiences happy and relaxed forever.

The steps may take longer if the dog has learned to grab the leash in his mouth or fight against the tension, but if you persevere they will still work.

Training Steps;

1. With your dog on his leash, walk a couple of steps and if the leash stays slack say the command word ('walk nicely' or something similar. We will talk about the 'heel' command later, so probably the best word would be 'heel') you have chosen for an easy leash and click/ reward in quick succession.

2. If the leash is tight you may need to change direction a few times to engineer a slack leash. As soon as any tension vanishes from the leash, carry out the command/click/reward sequence. I sometimes find that by simply stopping, thus breaking the sequence of him pulling, is often enough to make him realize he shouldn't pull. Please don't get into the habit that some 'impatient people' seem to do, and pull the poor dog back with enough force to pull him over. The dog is keen and excited to be out walking and sniffing about. Given the chance he wants to go off and do his own thing. So please be patient and considerate.

3. Just as an added note here, command/click/reward is referred to above. If you are not familiar with clicker training, it basically means, as your dog performs a correct action, such as walk nicely you say the command word (so he knows to associate the action with the word). You then use a clicker to mark the behavior (you don't have to use a clicker, you can substitute this with the words 'good boy/girl'). You finally reward the behavior with a treat to begin with, so he associates his action with something good and positive.

4. Repeat and practice.

5. Gradually increase the time between when you issue the command, and when you reward. This will not only keep him keen to carry out the action, but make it easier when you eventually phase out giving food rewards

6. Again, remember the 'release command' at the end of the session. (If you have come to this part first, without reading about 'release commands', the release is basically as follows: After successfully completing a piece of training, let your dog know they have completed it by releasing them. This can be done in conjunction with the treat stage, and you simply say "finished", or something similar. Again this is discussed in more detail in another section.)

Teaching a Vizsla to walk easily on a leash will probably take 3 to 6 training sessions in a quiet area. It will then need practice in various areas, gradually increasing distractions, to become a flawless command. This will require exposure to roads and busy traffic. You will need to get to a point of teaching him to sit and wait at the road side until it is safe to cross.

The time-scale to positive results of this particular lesson depend on how the dog has learned to walk on a leash in his life experiences so far.

Chapter Six:

Training Your Vizsla Dog

In this next chapter we will cover specific step by step obedience training methods for your Vizsla. The Vizsla is a very intelligent breed that typically responds well to training but he can be easily distracted sometimes. For the best success, you should plan to keep your training sessions short and fun so that your Vizsla gets something out of them each time. In addition to receiving step-by-step instructions for training your Vizsla dog, you will also learn the basics about different training methods.

1.) Popular Training Methods

When it comes to training your Vizsla you have a variety of training methods to choose from. Some of the most common training methods include positive reinforcement, punishment-based, alpha dog, and clicker training. In this section you will receive an overview of each training method as well as a recommendation for which option is best for your Vizsla.

a.) Positive-Reinforcement Training

One of the most popular training methods for dogs today is positive reinforcement training. This type of training is a version of operant conditioning in which the dog learns to associate an action with a consequence. In this case, the term consequence does not refer to something bad, it is just something that happens as a result of something else. The goal of positive reinforcement training is to encourage your dog to WANT to do what you want him to do.

The basics of positive reinforcement training are simple, you teach the dog that if he follows your commands he will be rewarded. For example, you teach your dog to respond to the word "Sit" by him sitting down. In order to teach him to associate the command with the action, you reward him with a treat each time he sits on command. It generally only takes a few repetitions for dogs to learn to respond to commands because food rewards are highly motivational for most dogs.

The key to successful positive reinforcement-based training sessions is to keep them short and fun. If the dog enjoys the training, he will be more likely to retain what he has learned. It is also important that you make the connection between the command and the desired response very clear to your dog. If he doesn't understand what you want him to do he will become confused. It is also important to pair the reward immediately with the desired response. This helps your dog to make the connection more quickly and it motivates him to repeat the desired behavior.

b.) Punishment-Based Training

Punishment-based training is not as harsh as the word suggests. It is not exactly the opposite of positive reinforcement training, but it is very different. While positive reinforcement training is about encouraging your dog to repeat a desired behavior, punishment-based training is about discouraging your dog from performing an unwanted behavior. The goal of punishment-based training is to teach your dog that a certain action results in a negative consequence and thus the dog will choose not to perform that behavior in the future.

The problem with punishment-based training methods is that it is generally only effective in teaching your dog to stop doing something rather than teaching him to respond to a certain command. It is also important to note that punishment-based training can have a negative impact on your relationship with your dog. Even though your dog may stop performing the unwanted behavior, it may not be because you taught him that the behavior is undesirable. He will likely only associate the behavior with fear and pain (depending on the type of punishment you use).

In addition to learning not to perform the behavior in question, your dog will also learn to be fearful of you. If you know anything about dog behavior, you may already know that, in most cases, aggression is born of fear. Even the most even-tempered dog can become aggressive if he is afraid. If you use punishment-based training methods you not only risk teaching your dog to fear you, but there is also the possibility that he will become aggressive with you at some point in the future.

Note: I would like to point out here, that if you adopt this style of training, you should NEVER, under any circumstances hit your dog. It is not only cruel, but an unnecessary action on your part. If you are ever having recurring behavioral issues with your dog, you should either seek an alternative approach or in extreme cases, seek the help of a professional dog trainer.

C.) Alpha Dog Training

You may be familiar with this style of training in conjunction with the ***"Dog Whisperer," Cesar Millan.*** Cesar Millan is a famous dog trainer who has published a number of books including three New York Times best sellers. Mr Millan's dog training methods are based on the idea that dogs are pack animals and that the dog owner must establish himself as leader of the pack. In doing so, the dog will become submissive and will submit to the owner's will.

According to Cesar Millan's style of training, you should never let your dog walk through a doorway before you and he must wait until you've finished your meal to receive his dinner. Though Mr Millan has a great many followers, there are also many who believe his training methods to be extreme and inhumane. In fact, the RSPCA issued a statement saying that "Adverse training methods which have been seen to be used by Cesar Millan can cause pain and fear for dogs and may worsen their behavioral problems". It is not my intention to discredit Mr Millan or his methods and I cannot personally comment about the effectiveness of his methods. If you are at all interested in this or any other approach, then I urge you to do your own research and make your own mind up. Again, providing you act with kindness, are firm but fair in your dog training approach, then I am sure you will have success which ever method you use.

D.) Clicker Training

Clicker training, as described in a previous chapter, is a type of positive reinforcement training. With this type of training you use a small clicker device to help your dog form an association with a command and the desired behavior. Because this is the most difficult part of positive reinforcement training, clicker training is often a very quick and effective training method. To use this method you follow the same procedures as you would for positive reinforcement training but you click the clicker as soon as your dog performs the desired behavior and then give him the reward. Once your dog identifies the desired behavior you then stop using the clicker so he does not become dependent on it.

E. Training Recommendations

It is completely your decision which training method you choose to utilize with your Vizsla but most dog trainers recommend some form of positive reinforcement training. Vizslas are a very intelligent breed so they typically pick things up fairly quickly. Using a clicker may help you to speed up your training sessions as well.

2.) House-Training Your Vizsla

This is covered in a previous chapter, but is used here in conjunction with crate training

When you bring home a Vizsla puppy, one of the first things you must do is house-train him. Puppies have very little control over their bladders and bowel movements, so house-training can sometimes be tricky. If you use the crate training method however, you can not only reduce the frequency of accidents, but you may also find that your puppy becomes house-trained fairly quickly. All you need to crate train your puppy is, of course, the crate, patience and some time.

You have already learned a little bit about the benefits of crating your puppy but in this section you will receive more detailed information about the crate training method. In order for this method to work, your puppy's crate, needs to be just big enough for him to stand, sit, lie down, and turn around in comfortably. If it is too much larger, your puppy might give in to the temptation, and have a toilet accident. You also need to understand that puppies cannot hold their bladders for more than a few hours until they reach six months old. So do not force your puppy to remain in the crate for longer than he can physically restrain himself.

Before you actually begin crate training your puppy you need to get your puppy used to the crate. If you skip this step in the process, your puppy may learn to associate the crate with bad things, such as you leaving the house. Instead, you should teach your Vizsla puppy that the crate is a good thing.

To do this you can follow these steps:

1. Take the door off the crate, if possible, or prop it open so that it does not close while your puppy is in it.

2. Bring your puppy over to the crate and talk to him

in a soothing voice as he explores it.

3. Toss a few treats in and around the crate to encourage your puppy to go inside of his own free will. If treats don't work, try a favorite toy.

4. Start feeding your puppy his meals in the crate. Ideally you should place his food bowl in the back of the crate so he has to go all the way in to eat.

5. Once your puppy is comfortable eating his meals in the crate, you can start to close the door while he is in it. Open the door again as soon as he is finished eating.

6. Each time you feed your puppy in the crate, leave the door closed a few minutes longer until your puppy remains in the crate for 10 minutes after eating.

7. Once your puppy gets used to this, you can start leaving the room for a few minutes after he has already been in the crate for 5 minutes.

8. Slowly increase the amount of time you spend away from your puppy while he is in the crate. If he starts whining or crying, you may have increased the duration of your absence too quickly.

Once your puppy is able to remain in the crate quietly for 30 minutes you can begin crate training. The process of crate training is really quite simple. Your overall aim is to leave your puppy in the crate overnight and when you leave the house. While you are at home, give him plenty of opportunities to do his business outside. If your puppy never has the opportunity to have an accident inside the housc, then crate training will not be a chore. It is possible that during the night, your puppy may need to do his toilet business. In this case I would advise lining the crate with newspaper of puppy pads. Most dogs I have known will bark, asking to go out. If it is possible, please do attend to the dog as it will be uncomfortable for him to be expected to hold this until the morning. If you prefer not to keep your dog in his crate overnight then leave him somewhere such as a kitchen with a tiled floor and again plenty of newspaper/puppy pads that can easily be cleaned up.

Follow the steps below to properly toilet train your puppy in conjunction with crate training:

Once again, I realize that details of the following have been covered previously. I apologize for repeating certain steps again. The point is, that when you first bring your puppy home you will need to start toilet training but will not necessarily immediately start him with crate training. You are now utilizing the crate and need to be aware of how this fits in conjunction with toilet training.

1. Choose an area of the yard where you want your puppy to do his business. House-

training will be easier if your puppy learns what you expect of him when you take him outside to that particular area.

2. Take your puppy outside to the special area every hour or so to give him a chance to do his business. If he doesn't go, take him right back inside. The reason you take him back inside straight away and not leave him to his own devices, is so he knows that this is training.

3. When you take your puppy outside and lead him to the special area, give him a verbal command like "go pee", "outside for a wee wee", or "toilets" etc. It is a good idea to choose and use the same command until he gets the idea. Using several different commands may confuse him. Once your puppy is successfully house-trained you'll be able to just open the door and give him the command. Eventually, your puppy will also get to the point where he stands at the door and gives a little bark, asking to go out.

4. If your puppy does his business, praise him excitedly and offer him a treat. Be very consistent about this to make sure your puppy learns what you expect of him.

5. When you are inside, keep your puppy confined to whatever room you are currently in. This will help to reduce the chance of accidents.

6. If you notice your puppy sniffing the ground or turning in circles, it is a sign that he has to go and you should take him outside before he has an accident.

7. Place your puppy in the crate overnight and when you are away from home so he doesn't have an accident. Hopefully at this point, he will know exactly what is expected, and be able to refrain from needing to go until the morning. However, if you are woken in the early hours, with his short, "asking to go out", bark, he may need letting outside. Please don't ignore this, as it will likely be uncomfortable for him to have to hold it until the morning.

8. For the first few weeks you will need to let your puppy out every few hours until he is old enough to hold his bladder overnight. If you work a full-time job you may need to ask a friend to stop by or hire a dog sitter.

9. Let your puppy outside immediately after releasing him from the crate, and always give him a chance to go before you put him in it.

If you follow these simple steps you will find that house-training your Vizsla puppy is really quite easy. In many cases, house-training only takes a few weeks. The key is to be as consistent as possible in letting your puppy outside as frequently as you can and in rewarding your puppy for doing his business outside. Your puppy has a natural desire to please you, so praising him for doing his business outside will teach him that you like that behavior and he will be eager to repeat it.

3.) Obedience Training - Teaching Basic Commands

While your puppy may not be able to comprehend complex commands right away, you should be able to start basic obedience training at a fairly young age. There are five main commands which form the basics of obedience training; Sit, Down, Come, Stay and Heal. In this section you will receive step-by-step instructions for teaching your Vizsla these five basic commands.

However, before we get started with those basic training commands I want to firstly remind/introduce you to a couple of useful preliminary aspects of his training.

A.) The Release Command

This is covered in another chapter, but again, if you are coming to this section first, then an explanation is in order. The 'release command' is particularly useful for a number of reasons. It first of all lets your dog know that he has successfully completed a part of his training. It also has a safety aspect to it, for example if you come to the edge of a busy road that you wish to cross. In this instance, you would have your dog sit until it is safe to cross. You then issue the release command to cross the road.

So, it is important to teach this from the moment that you start teaching your dog anything new at all. The release command is, as mentioned in a previous chapter, a word or words that you use at the end of each session or piece of training to let him know the training has finished. This can be, 'finished", 'all over', 'training over', or something similar. But again please be consistent here with the term you use.

B.) Focus On Me

We teach ***"focus"*** as a preliminary command for a very specific reason. A dog that is focused elsewhere is less likely to pay any attention to your requests.

When a dog is focusing on you, the other commands are much easier to teach.

Similarly the dog is far easier to control, when he is not focused on the rest of the environment.

<u>Training Steps:</u>

1. Take a really tempting treat and place it at the end of your dog's nose so that you have his attention. You may find you have to pinch it between your fingers incase he is tempted to snatch

it. Or let him sniff it, and then hold it in your hand, so that he knows it is there, but can't take it.

2. Move the treat gradually away from the dog and over your head; making sure that the dog's eyes are following your hand.

3. Bring the treat down at the back of your head in order for your dog's eyes to meet yours.

4. At the moment your eyes meet, say the command that you will use for asking your dog to focus, so for example say 'focus'. You then click if you are using the clicker method or say good boy/girl to mark the behavior and finally give him the treat. All of this needs to be done in very quick succession in the beginning, almost all at the same time.

5. Again, if he has completed this successfully, give him the release command. With the release command, you can just use this at the very end of the training session. However, in the initial stages of training I prefer to use it often and therefore make this habitual as soon as possible.

6. Repeat and practice.

7. Gradually increase the time between command, act and click/reward delivery. In this way he will retain focus longer and longer, until you finally give him the reward.

8. Practice, then eventually begin to use variable reward; that is, you gradually phase out giving him a treat, but always praise him with 'good boy' or whatever your praise word is.

Teaching a Vizsla to focus on you will probably take 3 to 5 training sessions in a quiet area. It will then need practice in various areas, such as a park with more dogs about. Therefore gradually increasing distractions, until it becomes a flawless command.

C.) Sit

For the dog that sits naturally, it is simple to capture the behavior with a click (or "good boy/girl"). Whilst it is also possible to easily lure the act, so that the dog is in the sit position.

This is a position that comes so naturally to a dog that most Vizsla dogs, as they are so naturally intelligent, will pop into the sit position if you show them something that they want.

As previously noted, this command is the best one to start with because sitting is a natural behavior your dog performs anyway. All you have to do is teach him to do it on command.

To teach your dog to sit on command, follow these steps:

1. Kneel in front of your Vizsla and hold a small treat in your dominant hand. Pinch the treat between your thumb and forefinger so your puppy can see it.

2. Hold the treat directly in front of your Vizsla's nose and give him a second to smell it.

3. Say "Sit" in a firm and even tone then immediately move the treat forward, away from you, toward the back of your dog's head. I prefer to keep saying the word sit until he sits. This is a technique known as leading, in that you lead your dog to perform the required action.

4. Your dog should lift his nose to follow the treat and, in doing so, his bottom should lower to the floor.

5. As soon as your dog's bottom hits the ground, click with your clicker or praise him excitedly with good boy/girl to mark the behavior and finally give him the treat.

6. Quickly release your dog, (remember the release word previously noted) repeat and practice.

7. Repeat this sequence several times until your puppy gets the hang of it.

8. Once your puppy does get the hang of the sequence, you should not have to lead anymore and just say 'sit' and he should sit.

9. If after all this, you find that he doesn't seem to be getting the idea, you can apply gentle pressure to the top of his hips, all the while saying 'sit'. This should hopefully encourage him to sit down.

10. Gradually increase the time between command, act and click/reward delivery. In this way he will retain focus longer and longer, until you finally give him the reward.

Teaching a Vizsla to sit in this way will probably take 1 to 3 training sessions in a quiet area then it will need practice in various areas. Gradually increase distractions, to become a flawless command.

D.) DOWN

Teaching a dog to lie down is another useful command. This can be used for anything from settling your dog when visitors come to the home, right through to telling him to drop at distance in an emergency.

The easiest way to teach a dog the down position initially is to lure the position. After a few goes, he will be offering to get into the position very quickly if he thinks you have something he may want. To get the initial idea through a lure is a pretty flawless method.

What you are effectively doing is to take a treat and pop it onto the end of your dog's nose and lure him to the ground. Here, you are drawing the treat down to the ground. It usually works in between his legs or as near as.

Again, once you have taught your Vizsla to sit, teaching him to lie down is the next logical step.

To teach your dog to lie down on command, follow these steps:

1. Kneel in front of your Vizsla and hold a small treat in your dominant hand – pinch the treat between your thumb and forefinger so your puppy can see it.

2. Hold the treat directly in front of your Vizsla's nose and give him a second to smell it.

3. Give your puppy the "Sit" command and wait for him to comply.

4. Once your puppy sits, immediately move the treat quickly down to the floor in between your puppy's front paws. It is important at this point to add the word "Down", or "Lie Down". I often prefer to keep repeating the word "Down", so that he hears it often enough to know that this new action relates to the word.

5. Your puppy should lie down to get the treat. If he does, again mark this with a click or praise him excitedly and give him the treat.

6. If your puppy stands up instead of lying down, calmly return to the beginning and repeat the sequence.

7. Again, once he successfully carries out the command, quickly release your dog, (remember the release word previously noted) repeat and practice.

8. Repeat this sequence several times until your puppy gets the hang of it.

9. You should be able to get to the point of skipping the 'sit' command and simply say 'Lie Down', to get the desired action from him.

10. There are some extra options for the dog that is simply not getting the idea. You can sit on a chair and lure your Vizsla under your outstretched leg. What this does is to make him crawl under your leg, which should leave him in the down position.

11. Be patient here, but if after countless attempts, nothing seems to be working then try the following. As you go through the sequence above, if his back end is sticking up in a beg position, gently apply some pressure to his hips. As you gently push down say the words, 'down' or 'lie down'. Again, as soon as he does it, and doesn't immediately get up, click or praise to mark the behavior and reward.

Teaching a Vizsla to lie down will usually take 3 to 6 short training sessions in a quiet area. You will then need to practice in various areas, gradually increasing distractions, to become a flawless command.

E.) Come

Teaching your dog to come to you when called is incredibly important. Say, for instance, that you open the front door of your house one day and your Vizsla rushes out before you can stop him. Your dog does not understand the danger of a busy street but if you have taught him to come to you when called, you can save him from that danger.

The Vizsla needs to be taught to come back when called as soon as possible and in careful stages.

Most dogs can either be super responsive to recall or happy to leave you standing all day, calling his name in vain, whilst he chases rabbits or squirrels around the park. Regardless of his behavior outdoors though, this breed really needs a free run every day in order to be truly healthy.

Even the very best behaved pet that is happy to settle in the home, whether he has been for a run or not, will suffer if he isn't given the opportunity to stretch his muscles. A bored Vizsla dog can easily become depressed, destructive or even aggressive.

Owners give many reasons for not giving a Vizsla the free run that he needs, most of the reasons are fear in one way or another. The main concern is that the dog owner is scared of their pet running away and never coming back.

Recall training can be broken down into easy steps and recall games added to strengthen the behavior. The exact same approach is taken when teaching recall as when teaching anything else to the dog. You always set the dog up to succeed; never allow room for failure; therefore building his confidence high.

With recall you need to make certain that your dog sees you as the most interesting and attractive prospect in the area. If you are red faced and shouting his name with frustration he is less likely to want to come back. He will naturally think you are angry with him.

There are some very specific habits that you can procure when teaching recall;

Ideally you should allow your dog off the lead to run or do recall training in an isolated area and certainly not near a busy road were there is a risk of him running across the road and possibly being run over. Always be on your guard to potentially hazardous areas and therefore avoid accidents. I once had a situation with an Irish Setter that took off across a field after it had picked up the scent of something. I literally shouted my head off and fortunately she came to her senses and came running back. Dogs can easily give chase to rabbits and if you are near a road there is a chance the rabbit may cross, along with your dog. Please pre-empt and avoid this from happening. If in doubt, keep your dog on a long lead.

If you get a situation as described above, never punish your dog when he gets to you. Always be welcoming and friendly, no matter how frustrated you are, or he may not come back at all next time.

Never chase your dog. The only time you should give chase is if an emergency situation is apparent. If possible run the other way if he is ignoring you. By being the most interesting thing in the area and rapidly disappearing into the distance you are most likely to attract the attention of your Vizsla. Giving chase can be seen a game for the dog and you giving chase adds to their excitement.

Set up positive results. When your dog is looking for the next thing to do this is the best time to call him and show the treat. Yes, it's trickery but it will convince the dog that he comes to you each time you call.

Whether your dog is ten weeks or ten years old, puppy recall steps will work in the same way.

For complete success it is vital not to move on from the present step unless it is absolutely 100% learned and established.

Remember we are aiming for success even if we have to manipulate it at first.

Whether you have never allowed your dog off his leash or he runs away every time you do, these stages will help. It is much better to go too slowly though. You want to avoid giving your dog the idea of running away.

<u>To teach your dog to come to you on command, follow these steps:</u>

1. Work out an extra motivator involving your clicker and some tasty treats of course. Also carry a squeaky toy or something of equal fascination to your dog. Save the toy for recall and only allow short play periods and limited use by your dog. This will ensure that it is a "magic toy" in his mind. Again, the thing to bare in mind is that it needs to make him keen enough to want it.

2. I would always advise you to do this in a secluded open field, preferably away from any road. You may have success with this in a secluded part of a park field, perhaps early morning. It is also a great idea to get hold of one of those long retractable leads or a10 meter plus training lead. That way you can let him off at some distance, but you still have him safely attached, in case he decides to take off.

3. Now simply let him go off, all the while allowing the lead to extend. Stop, and call him back with your recall command (I would advise using his name along with 'come' or 'come on' or 'come here'). As he is heading back towards you use a click/praise then take his collar and give him the treat, and always use the release command.

4. It is vital to take the dog's collar every time you give him the treat because this prevents the act of 'grab and run'. Do not be tempted to ask your dog to sit or do anything else at this point, he came to you and this is enough for now, adding extra commands is adding pressure to the recall command and may put your dog off.

5. Only when your dog is coming back every single time using the extended leash, enlist the help of a friend. Your helper is going to hold your dog and you are going to show the dog a treat. Take a few steps away and call the dog. Your helper is then going to release him as you call. As he runs toward you, click/praise, take his collar and treat in exactly the same way. Release him as before.

6. Then, when the above steps are established you can increase the distance that you go before the dog is released, you can start to run away and hide. Eventually you can start to allow the dog off leash and practice calling him back a few times each walk.

This whole process may take a few weeks but do not be tempted to let your dog off the long leash too soon as he may ignore your call and this can easily develop into a habit of running away.

F.) Stay

After you have taught your dog to come to you on command, the next logical step is to teach him the opposite – to stay or wait until you call him.

To teach your dog to stay on command, follow these steps:

1. Kneel in front of your Vizsla and hold a small treat in your dominant hand. Pinch the treat between your thumb and forefinger so your puppy can see it.
2. Hold the treat directly in front of your Vizsla's nose and give him a second to smell it.
3. Give your puppy the "Sit" command and wait for him to comply.
4. Now say "Stay" in a firm, even tone and take a step or two backward away from your puppy.
5. Pause for a second then walk back up to your puppy. Now click/praise to mark the fact that he has stayed put. Finally reward him with a treat. You do not want to release him until you have walked back and he has successfully remained seated throughout.
6. Repeat the sequence several times, rewarding your puppy each time he stays.
7. Each time you practice this, aim to increase the distance between you and your dog. You can measure this in paces if you like, so two steps to four, then eight and so on. Once I get some distance between me and the dog, I like to add the release so that he comes back to me. So start him in the sit position as before and say 'stay'. I usually keep repeating this as I walk backward. Once you have walked back quite a few paces, stop and pause as long as you feel he is concentrating. Then call him back to you, with 'come on [his name]', praise and give him the treat as before.

G.) Heel

Teaching a Vizsla to heel is easy. I always teach walking to heel with him on a leash first then off leash in a safe area. To a certain extent, you will probably have already introduced him to this in the early training as mentioned previously when you started him on his walks. We will extend and add to that training here.

When you are teaching a dog to walk to heel it is important that you focus on the position and never on the leash.

To keep pulling the dog back from a tense leash, to a slack one, whilst stating the command to heel will never work, because the dog is not actually learning anything with this approach.

Training Steps;

1. Some people prefer to start the puppy in a sit, stay position, and then move to either the right or left hand side of the dog.

2. It is important that you have the loop of the lead through whichever is your preferred lead hand, so it hangs on your wrist. Your puppy should then be on the opposite side to that. So if you hold the loop of the lead in your right hand, have the dog walk at your left side. This is more for control and safety of your puppy in these initial stages. With the other hand, in this case your left, grip the lead, so that it is close to your dog, giving you greater control. This will also act as a guide or restraint to let your puppy know where you want him, should your puppy surge forward or hang back.

3. Next give the command to "heel", whilst starting to walk. Hopefully your puppy will follow you at your side. All the while say the command "heel", not just once, but keep repeating this.

4. If at this point your puppy has walked with you, without surging in front or lagging behind, and staying at your side; then you can stop click/praise to mark the behavior and again give him his treat. That is the

ideal scenario. However if he doesn't do that, simply stop and start again.

5. Remember, at what ever point he successfully walks at heel and you have praised him, release him before you continue.

6. Now do exactly as before, only this time try and go further, perhaps walking several feet or yards. Again stop when you are satisfied he has improved and as before, click/praise, reward and release.

7. Eventually you will have him walking nicely at your side without pulling forward or holding back.

When you've completed the session, praise your dog with your usual release command, indicating that you have finished, so that he understands he has been successful, you are pleased and that training is over.

Once again, when training a young puppy who pulls strongly at the leash, you'll need to stand still until your pup understands that he's not going anywhere until he listens. Once your puppy understands that he only receives praise when he begins to respond appropriately, it will only take a few days before he's walking right next to you without pulling on the lead.

Once you get him successfully walking at your side, you can increase the difficulty of the exercise by suddenly turning at a right angle, or do a complete about turn. This is more or less what happens in agility training and dog shows. The dog follows precise paths at your side.

As mentioned at the beginning, you can increase the level of difficulty with this exercise by eventually practicing this without the lead. However, only try this in a safe area, and certainly not near a busy road.

Teaching a Vizsla to walk nicely at heel will probably take 4 to 6 training sessions in a quiet area. It will then need practice in various areas, gradually increasing distractions, to become a flawless command.

If you follow the steps listed previously, teaching your puppy to respond to the five basic commands should not be a difficult or lengthy process. Make sure to keep your training sessions short. Only about 10 or 15 minutes to ensure that your puppy stays engaged. If he starts to get bored or distracted in the middle of a session, stop for now and pick it up again later.

4.) Incorporating Hand Signals

Once your Vizsla is consistently responding to the five basic commands you can start to incorporate hand signals. The process is a little bit different for each command, but you should be able to follow the same basic steps to incorporate a hand signal. Make sure that the hand signal you choose for each command is easily distinguishable from the others so your dog doesn't get confused.

Follow these steps to incorporate hand signals:

1. Kneel in front of your Vizsla and hold a small treat in your non-dominant hand.

2. Hold your other hand in front of your puppy's nose as if you were holding a treat.

3. When you have your puppy's attention, give the "Sit" command and shape your hand into a fist then move it forward toward the back of your puppy's head just as you did earlier with the treat in hand.

4. When your puppy's bottom touches the ground, click/praise as before, release him and praise excitedly and offer him the treat from your other hand

5. Repeat this sequence several times until your puppy responds consistently and associates the fist/hand signal with the sit command.

Use this same process to teach your dog a hand signal for the "Down" command. Holding your hand out flat, parallel to the floor, move the palm up and down while you say the word "Down" or lie down

For "Stay", I would recommend holding your palm flat and as near vertical as possible towards your dog. This is not dissimilar to a traffic officer holding out their palm to get motorists to stop.

Again taking the traffic officer analogy, use the same signal they use to beckon traffic towards them, for when you need him to "Come to you".

For the "heel" command I usually pat/slap the side of my leg to indicate, that is where you want him to be.

Once you have taught your puppy to respond to hand signals as well as verbal commands you can move on to the next step which is to phase out the food rewards.

5.) Phasing Out Food Rewards

Food is a highly motivating reward for dogs but you do not want your Vizsla to become dependent on a food reward indefinitely to perform the desired behavior. Once your puppy starts to respond consistently with the right behavior, when you give him a command, you should start phasing out the treats. Start by only rewarding your puppy every other time then cut it back to every third time and so on. Even though you are phasing out the food rewards you still need to praise your puppy so he knows that you are pleased with him. You may even choose to substitute a food reward for a toy and give your puppy a brief play session with the toy as a reward instead of the treat.

6.) Swapping

If you are training any dog, then it is a good idea to teach swapping very early on.

Every dog should know how to swap because this is a good and fair way to take something away from the dog that he shouldn't have. Obviously if this is something dangerous to the dog, then I would not recommend being so polite. In an emergency you would have to snatch this immediately and take it out of harms way. However, in non dangerous situations, proceed as follows.

1. Whilst your dog is playing with a toy, have another one to hand

2. Offer the new toy in front of him, say the word 'leave' or 'swap'; you may have to repeat the command word until he drops it.

3. Hopefully he drops the one he has, ready to take the one you have. At the point he drops it click/praise, and reward; allowing him to carry on with the new toy.

Retrieving with balls is a really good way to practice this. You can show the dog that you are happy to throw the next ball just as soon as he has handed over the one he just fetched back.

If your dog doesn't want to give something to you then you can change your approach and convince him that the item is pretty much worthless. If he thinks you don't care about an item then your dog is far less likely to care about it either. Even the most precious thing often loses value very quickly with lack of human interest.

7.) Further Training

There are many options for further training with the Vizsla. The choices are endless for sports and fun classes, particularly for the fit and healthy members of the breed.

On that note, it is vital that you ensure your own dog's joints are sound before asking too much of him physically.

Sporty dogs can join agility classes, flyball teams and even CaniX, where owners run with their dogs. All of these are great fun and perfect for the more active dogs and owners amongst us.

Flyball is a team relay that includes a mixture of hurdles and speed.

Agility is a sport where the dog encounters a series of hurdles, weaves and similar obstacles in a timed race against the clock. The sport is great fun and a lot of dogs excel at agility.

Competitive obedience is an art where the dog is taught sharp obedience that looks great in a show ring. The more modern forms are heel-work to music or dancing with dogs. You will no doubt find that your dog makes an enthusiastic obedience partner.

Therapy dogs, a job for the older steadier pet, are assessed and taken into homes and hospitals at visiting times. If your dog is kind and you want to do more with him, or her, then registering them as a therapy dog will change both of your lives.

Chapter Seven:

Grooming Your Vizsla

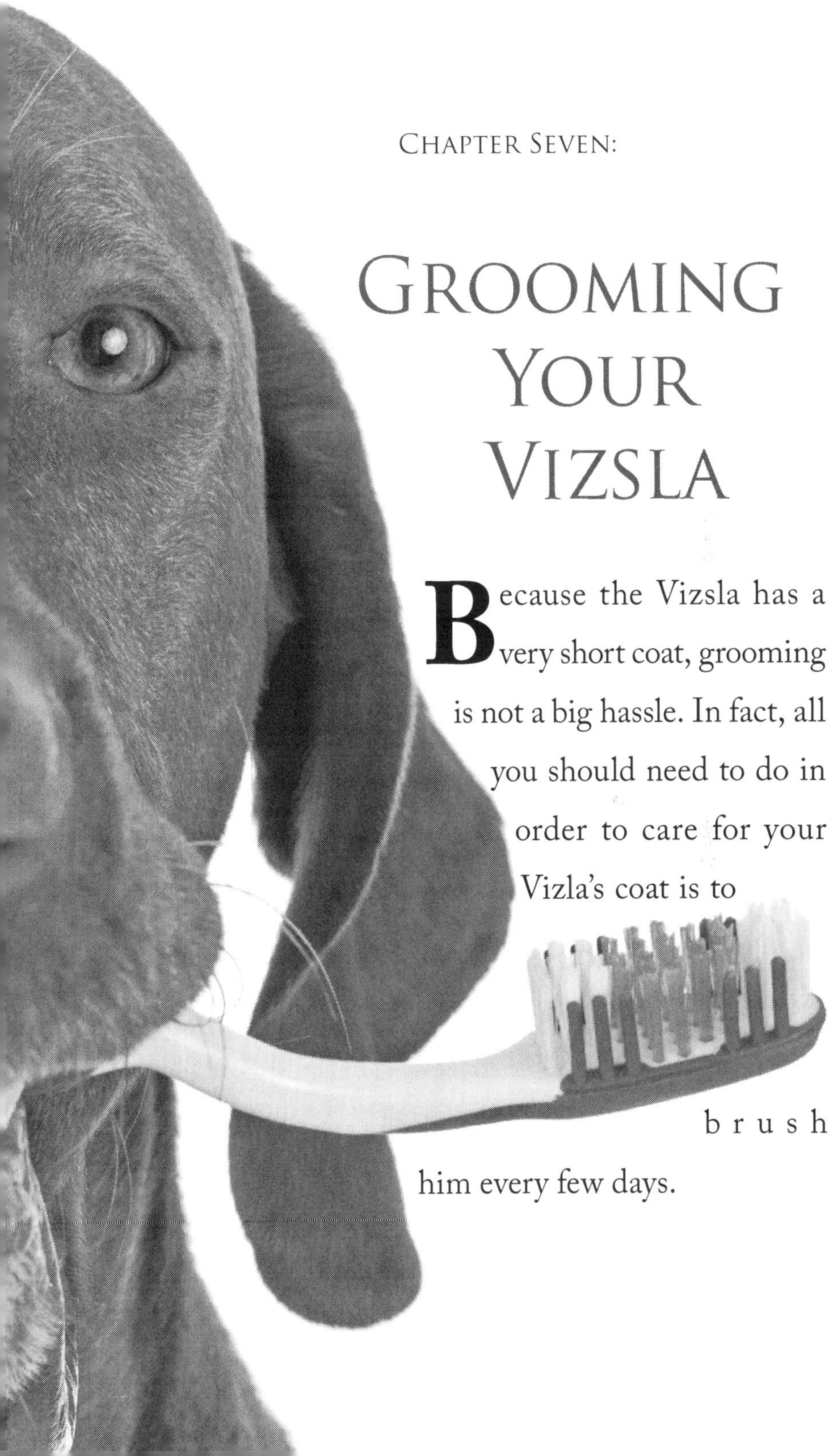

Because the Vizsla has a very short coat, grooming is not a big hassle. In fact, all you should need to do in order to care for your Vizla's coat is to brush him every few days.

Not only does grooming help to control shedding but it also helps to ensure that your dog's coat and skin remain healthy. In this chapter you will learn the basics about grooming your Vizsla including tips for cleaning your dog's ears, brushing his teeth, and trimming his nails.

1.) Tools and Methods

Some dogs do not react well to grooming because they do not like being held still. Because grooming is so important however, you should get your puppy used to grooming from an early age. Brush your puppy for a few seconds at a time several times a day until he no longer seems bothered by it. Then you can cut back to one longer brushing session each day. You should also frequently touch your puppy's paws and ears so that once you start trimming his nails and cleaning his ears he will be used to this kind of handling. When grooming, always be gentle and brush or comb, with slow careful strokes. The last thing you want is for your dog to start shaking and be left traumatized, or the very least, disliking the experience.

Vizslas are generally a clean breed but they do need bathing occasionally, especially if they spend a lot of time outside.

To bathe your Vizsla at home follow the steps outlined below:

1. Give your Vizsla a good brushing before you bathe him to get rid of accumulated loose hair. You may even want to use an undercoat rake to thin out your dog's undercoat, particularly in the case of the Wirehaired Vizsla.

2. Fill your bathtub with a few inches of lukewarm water. You may also want to put down a rubber bath mat so your dog doesn't slip in the tub.

3. Place your Vizsla in the tub and wet down his fur with a handheld hose or by pouring water over him. You may need to use your hands to work the water all the way down to his skin.

4. Avoid getting your Vizsla's eyes and ears wet when you bathe him. Wet ears are a breeding ground for bacteria that could cause an ear infection.

5. Apply a small amount of mild dog-friendly shampoo to your Vizsla's back and gently work it into a lather, along his neck, back, chest and legs. Obviously avoid getting soap in his eyes, as you can imagine, it will sting.

6. Rinse the soap thoroughly out of your Vizsla's coat and use a damp washcloth to clean his face.

7. Use a large fluffy towel to towel-dry your Vizsla, get-

ting as much water out of his coat as possible. If it is warm outside or you have the central heating on, you can let him air-dry the rest of the way.

8. However, if your Vizsla seems to be cold you can use a hairdryer on the low heat setting to dry him. Unless it is a particularly warm summers day, I prefer to use a hair drier in any case.

You can bathe your Vizsla if he gets dirty, but you should avoid bathing him when it is not necessary. Over-bathing a dog can dry out his skin and lead to skin problems. In some cases you may be able to brush dry dirt and debris out of your Vizsla's coat instead of bathing him.

2.) Trimming Your Dog's Nails

Trimming your Vizsla's nails can be challenging because you need to be very careful. A dog's nail contains a quick; the vessel that brings blood to the nail. If you cut the nail too short you will cut the quick. This not only causes your dog pain, but it can bleed profusely as well. When you trim your Vizsla's nails you should only cut the very tip to remove the point. Depending on what color your dog's nails are, you may be able to see the quick and use it as a trimming guide.

It is generally recommended that you trim your Vizsla's nails every two weeks. If you do it this often, then you will only need to clip the slightest amount off the nail each time. This will reduce the risk of cutting the quick. Before you trim your Vizsla's nails for the first time you should consider having a veterinarian or a professional groomer show you how to do it properly. You also need to be sure you are using real dog nail clippers for the job. Please also

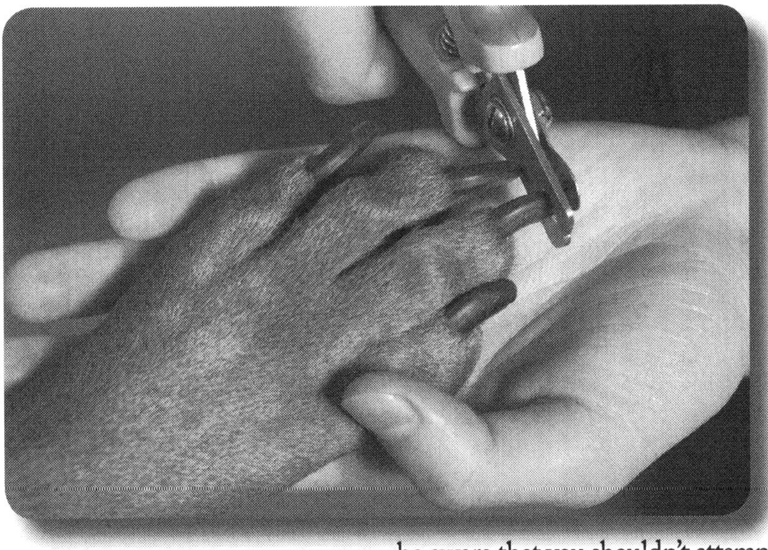

be aware that you shouldn't attempt to clip your dog's nails routinely every two weeks, just for the sake of it, as he may not need it. You should notice that if your dog walks on pavements or your concrete yard, he will to a certain extent be filing them down anyway.

3.) Cleaning Your Dog's Ears

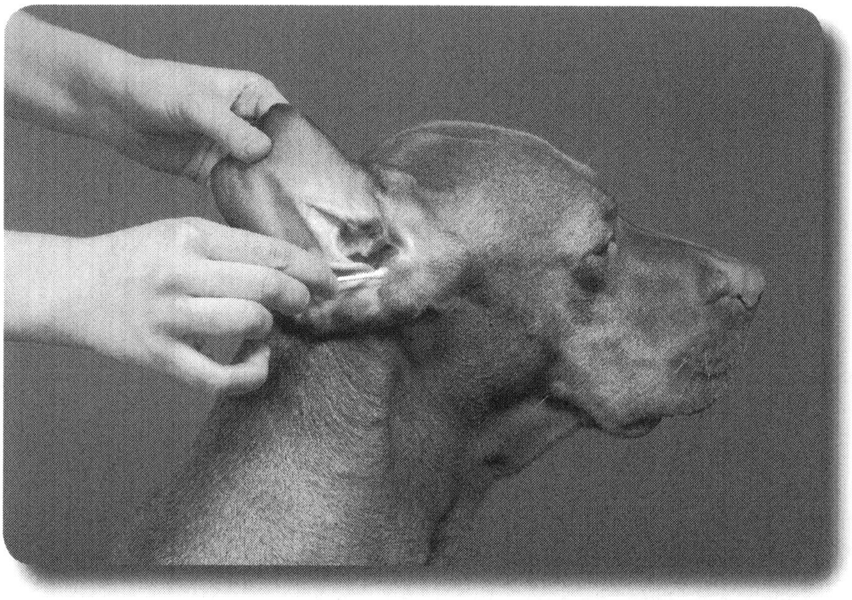

Because the Vizla's ears hang down over the sides of his head there is an increased risk for ear infections. Drop ears, like the Vizsla has, means that air and moisture get trapped under the flap of the ear, making it a breeding ground for bacteria. Your dog's risk of ear infection increases significantly if you get the ears wet, such as during a bath.

Cleaning your dog's ears is not difficult, but you do need the right supplies. Gear up with a bottle of dog-friendly ear cleaning solution and a few clean cotton balls. Gently lift your dog's ear and squeeze a few drops of the cleaning solution into the ear canal. Rub the base of your dog's ear with your fingers to spread the solution then use the cotton balls to wipe it away. Be careful not to put your fingers or the cotton ball too far into your dog's ear or you could damage his ear drum. The frequency with which you clean your Vizsla's ears will vary but you should aim for once every week or two. Please also note that the above photo is for illustration purposes only and I would only recommend using a cotton bud for light usage. Never attempt to go into the ear canal as the ear can be easily damaged.

4.) Brushing Your Vizsla's Teeth

The idea of brushing your dog's teeth may sound strange but dental health is just as important for your dog as it is for you. In fact, periodontitis (gum disease) is five times more common in dogs than in humans. Gum disease is incredibly serious but it often goes unnoticed by pet parents, especially since many people think that dogs are supposed to have bad breath. Bad breath, or halitosis, is one of the most common signs of gum disease and could be indicative of a tooth abscess. If you suspect anything un-toward, seek a veterinary examination as soon as possible.

To brush your Vizsla's teeth, follow the steps below:

1. Select a soft-bristle toothbrush to use. Most pet stores stock special toothbrushes for dogs.

2. Choose a toothpaste that is specifically made for dogs. They come in a variety of flavors, so select one your Vizsla will like. He will probably like them all. One important thing to add here; never use the tooth paste you use. These contain chemicals that can be harmful to dogs.

3. Get your dog used to having his teeth handled by gently placing your finger in his mouth against his teeth. Carefully manipulate his lips so he gets used to the feeling.

4. If you find he doesn't particularly like this, try dipping your finger in peanut butter or chicken broth so your dog learns to like the treatment.

5. When you are ready to brush, place one hand over your dog's mouth and gently pull back his lips.

6. Apply a small amount of toothpaste to the brush and rub it gently over a few of his teeth.

7. After a few seconds, stop brushing and give your Vizsla a treat for good behavior.

8. Slowly increase the length of your brushing sessions over a few days until your dog lets you brush all of his teeth in one session.

In addition to brushing your Vizsla's teeth at home you should also make sure he gets a dental checkup from the vet every 6 months.

Also consider giving your dog fresh beef bones on a regular basis. I would avoid the cooked variety as these can easily splinter and cause all sorts of internal intestinal problems. Unfortunately bones can cause intestinal problems and many people avoid them. If in doubt consider good quality dental sticks that are free from additives. They all help to keep dogs teeth and gums healthy.

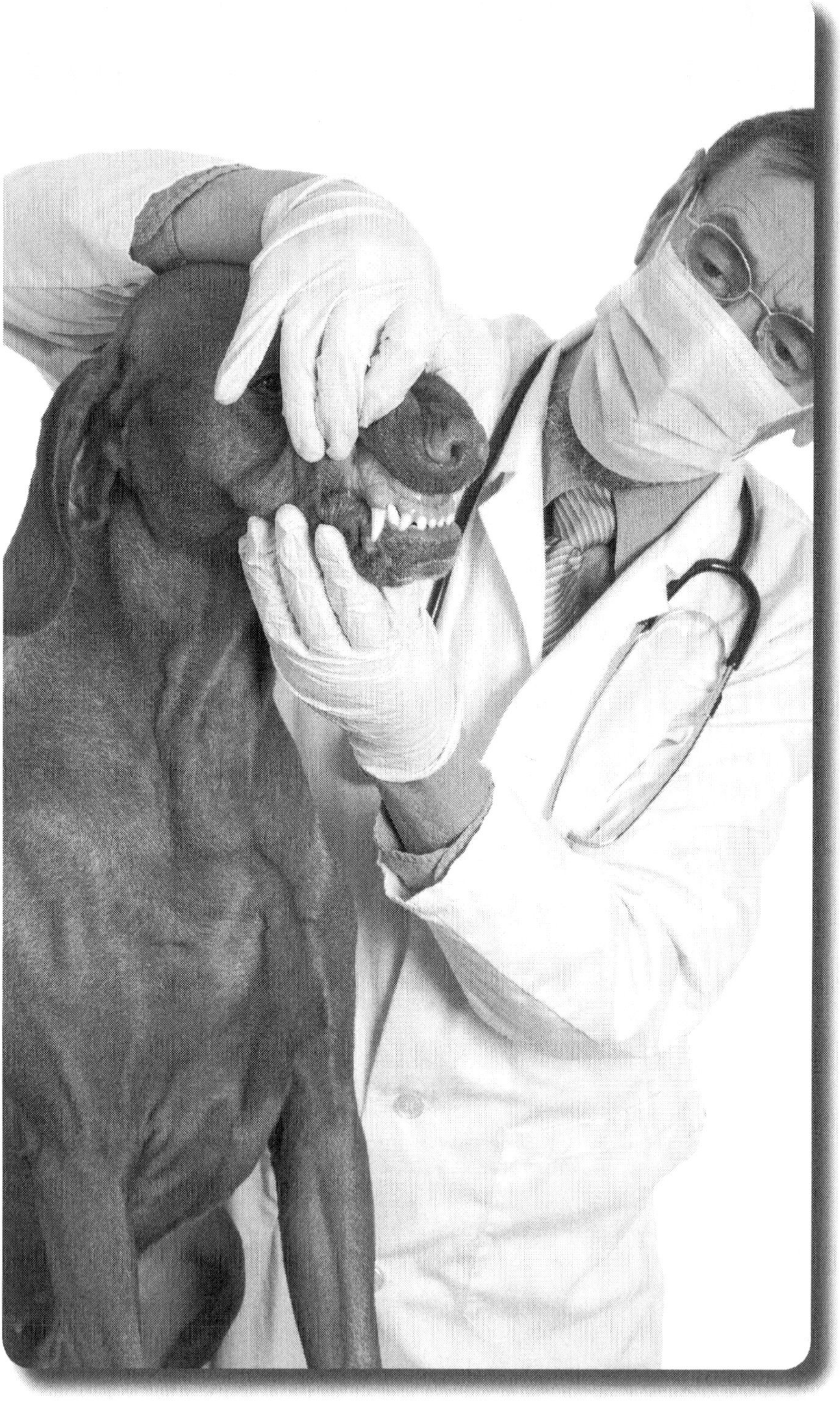

CHAPTER EIGHT:

HEALTH CHECKS AND FIRST AID

Before we get into the main health issues affecting the Vizsla, this chapter will deal with important preventive care. There is also useful and sometimes vital advice on health checks and first aid.

1.) Choosing a Veterinarian

You may already know this but not all veterinarians are the same. They are only people after all. So to find a good vet that you get on well with, may take some time and effort.

Dog owners in most geographical areas tend to gravitate towards a particular vet. It is usually someone who is good with dogs, trustworthy, great at the job and also has a good bedside manner with worried dog owners.

It is vitally important that you are completely happy with the vet that you choose for your dog. This person may need to lead you through some very difficult times. So a veterinarian who is hazy when sharing information or blunt towards you, may be very stressful for your entire family if you have an ill dog.

A good way to find a popular vet in your local area is do some community research, ask other dog walkers, go onto Facebook and find community pages of dog owners in your local area. Find out from other people what their experiences are and learn from them.

As holistic care is growing in popularity, a number of holistic veterinary surgeons are becoming available. This is an option that I personally would urge you to consider; though it is usually more expensive, it is well worth it.

The holistic vet has learned about veterinary science via the conventional route but has, in addition, put a lot of effort into learning natural health-care too. They will often treat symptoms with a mixture of less invasive therapies and conventional medicine, rather than simply use pharmaceutical options.

In short the holistic vet is more likely to look at the entire dog, diet, lifestyle and external influences on the health of your dog, as part of an overall holistic approach of care and treatment.

2.) Daily Health Check: Essential Handling

What Will Early Handling Establish?

Handling your dog early on will teach him that being touched and health checked is a perfectly normal part of his life. This makes life so much easier at the vets along with making nail clipping and similar activities stress free. Handling in this way will also give you the chance to see what is normal for your own dog and his health. This way you will be able to recognize and catch any problems quickly.

Physical Manipulation

If you live with a young puppy, lift the dog up and cradle him in your arms on his back. There is no real reason for this position other than it's quite a difficult place for a dog to relax in, because it exposes his belly. Therefore by enjoying it, he is learning to be relaxed when handled regardless of what is going on. You will probably not be able to manage this with older Vizsla. In this case you should really just attempt handling in whatever position is comfortable for them, whether sitting or lying them down on their back, or front. The important thing is that you handle them. Also be initially wary of an older rescue dog until you know that they do not mind you handling them..

Next take hold of each paw and look at the underside of the pads by squashing them open. This will help to check pads for cuts and foreign articles when you really need to. If you find any sharp object stuck in there, do your best to carefully pull this out preferably with tweezers. If this looks difficult, then you are probably best taking him to the vet, as soon as possible, to get them to extract it.

Ears

Take a good look into the dog's ears. They should be pink and clean with no thick or smelly discharge. Look out for signs of redness and swelling.

Try to make the ear examination similar to one he will have at the veterinary surgery. Again if you notice anything untoward, do not delay in taking him to the vet.

Eyes

Carefully examine your dog's eyes for swelling or redness. A small amount of sleep is normal. If you live with an adult or an older dog any blueness or blurring can be a sign of cataracts.

You can check your dog's sight by holding his face gently forward and dropping a balled up tissue or feather on the edge of his vision at each side of his head. If his vision is fine he will notice this straight away, if not, he may have a problem. Again a trip to the vets will be best for further investigation.

Teeth

Next check your dog's teeth right to the back of his mouth. As previously mentioned, it is a good idea to start brushing your dog's teeth early. If you are doing this on a daily basis, you will soon notice any problems that will need checking at the vets.

Feet

Then check each of the paws, checking the nails, and as previously mentioned, cut any that seem to have overgrown. We have already covered this to an extent in the chapter on grooming, but it is worth mentioning again.

The toenail of a dog is slightly different to that of a human so will need very careful handling. The nerve grows into the nail, which can easily be seen with white toenails but is more difficult with dark ones.

It is completely up to you whether you clip your own dog's nails or find a professional groomer or vet to do it. If you decide to clip them, then you will need to buy specific clippers and only take the very tip away with the clippers, or you may hurt the dog. If you would like to try this yourself, but are nervous at first, ask someone to show you or watch one of the many Youtube videos for instruction.

Anus and Genitals

After the feet, simply check the anus area and genitals for any abnormal discharge or swelling then finish by physically running your hands down the puppy's tail.

A.) The Worried or Reactive Vizsla

If you are bringing home an older Vizsla then it is important not to push your luck with handling. Remember that the dog will be confused and maybe even quite stressed.

A good way to carry out handling with a worried dog is to do it a few minutes, or even seconds if necessary, at a time and reward with treats, then stop.

The idea is to show the dog that handling and checking his ears, eyes and teeth etc, is a pleasant experience that brings nice food rewards.

Never force the worried dog beyond his limitations. Always stop whilst he is still relaxed and try to understand that this may all be brand new to him.

B.) Basic Massage and Muscle Care

Basic Massage can also be carried out when handling your dog of any age. By taking a few moments to first massage the dog's ears, where there are a lot of relaxing acupressure points, then moving your hands down his body in even strokes, you will be able to check his muscle balance and well-being.

Any uneven muscle balance will show that there is a potential skeletal problem below the surface. This is something that can be carefully monitored and should really be checked by the vet.

Any heat or swelling in the muscle areas may show a deeper problem. Similarly if the dog licks his lips, yawns or tries to move when you touch a certain area of his body then he could have some type of pain beneath the surface and is displaying calming signals as a response to your touch. It could also be nothing to worry about and the dog displays calming signals because they perhaps do not like been handled.

3.) First Aid

As the owner of a Vizsla dog it is a good idea to have at least a basic idea of canine first aid.

General first aid and its universal lesson is currently using the Acronym ***Dr's ABC.*** By memorizing this you have at least a basic idea of what to do if you ever find yourself in a first aid situation.

Danger

Remove the animal from any further danger, and be aware of danger to yourself in the situation.

Response

Check the response of the dog, is he conscious?

Summon help

Shout for help, ask someone to call the vet if possible.

Airway

Check the dog's airway, can he breathe? Is there an obstruction?

Breathing

At this point there may be a need to re-trigger breathing for the animal. Holding the mouth closed you can gently breath air into your dog's nostrils. Try to visualize the size of his lungs and not over inflate them, try to mimic how your dog would pant.

Cardiac compressions may be necessary at this point. The dog should be laid on his right side and the heart massaged in a similar way to CPR compressions for a human but carefully at a ratio of two breaths to one compression.

The heart is approximately located in the chest area above his left leg, is said to have a stronger beat on the left but can be felt on both sides.

Circulation

In an emergency, the dog's pulse and circulation will need to be checked. If bleeding is apparent then the wound will need to be put under pressure and elevated if possible in order to contain the bleeding.

After first aid has been carried out, the Vizsla should always be taken to see the vet as a matter of urgency.

There are some particular conditions that can develop very quickly can cause rapid health deterioration; which as a Vizsla owner it is important to be aware of. One of these is heat stroke or heat exhaustion.

4.) HEAT EXHAUSTION

Dogs can only pant to cool themselves as they don't sweat like people do; except to a certain extent from their paw pads.

In the warm summer months it is vital to keep your dog away from hot sun. Because he only cools his body on the inside by taking air from his surroundings, the dog in excessive heat, loses the power to cool himself at all. This will quickly lead to heat exhaustion which can be a fatal condition.

Dogs should never be left in hot cars, full sun or hot areas from which they cannot escape.

The symptoms of heat exhaustion are as follows;

Important!

* Panting (however, dogs do this naturally anyway and in most cases is not indicative of a problem)
* Restlessness
* Loss of focus in the eyes
* Deterioration of consciousness
* Staggering
* Collapse

If you suspect that your Vizsla dog is overheating it is vital never to take the panicked action of immersing him in cold water, as this can cause shock or even heart failure. Remove the dog from full sun and either drape damp towels over his body or dribble water over him to cool his overheated body gently.

When the body has overheated, then it is vital to get your dog checked by the vet for symptoms of long term damage.

A relatively new invention in the dog equipment world is the cooling vest. It can be placed in water then put onto the dog in hot weather.

The water wicks the heat away from the dogs body as a process of evaporation. If you believe that your dog is particularly susceptible to hot weather, then a cooling vest is a really good investment.

Another good idea for the warmer months is to provide your dog with a stock pot iced pop. Simply pour stock into a big bowl, add some treats of varying types and freeze the entire thing. Then on a hot day turn the ice pop out into the garden and allow your dog to lick away happily. You may want to place this on some sort of a tray in case the whole thing melts before he has chance to consume it.

5.) Essential Exercise

Every Vizsla dog needs daily walks, and will certainly not be happy at home all day. The adult Vizsla ideally needs at least 1-2 hours good running every single day or he will develop behaviors that cause you problems.

The first sign that your dog is not getting enough exercise is weight gain. There will also be the matter of excess energy that can easily cause destructive or even aggressive behavior.

Many dog behavior problems are sorted out very quickly when the dog's food is changed (food causing allergies or just poor food quality lacking necessary nutrients) and the daily walks are increased in time and intensity. Many of the most problematic behaviors stem from a lack of suitable exercise.

If you are out at work for a full day then why not consider a doggy day care or professional dog walker for your Vizsla dog. A good professional canine caretaker will wear your dog out and meet his social needs all at once.

Vizsla puppies need to be broken in gently to exercise, as their bones are soft whilst they are still growing. Your regular, long walks will begin when your puppy is a few months old.

Puppy exercise should involve gentle short walks; the UK Kennel

club advises;

"Puppies need much less exercise than fully-grown dogs. If you over-exercise a growing puppy you can overtire it and damage its developing joints, causing early arthritis. A good rule of thumb is a ratio of five minutes exercise per month of age (up to twice a day) until the puppy is fully grown, i.e. 15 minutes (up to twice a day) when three months old, 20 minutes when four months old etc. Once they are fully grown, they can go out for much longer.

It is important that puppies and dogs go out for exercise every day in a safe and secure area, or they may become frustrated. Time spent in the garden (however large) is no substitute for exploring new environments and socializing with other dogs. (Make sure your puppy is trained to recall so that you are confident that he will return to you when called)".

See more at: *http://www.thekennelclub.org.uk*

The Vizsla reaches adolescence at around 10 months old and adulthood, or maturity, comes quickly after-wards. So by the time your puppy is a year old he should be fine to walk as long as you like, within reason.

It is important that you still socialize your puppy throughout his first few months, simply by carrying him a lot of the time and putting him onto the ground to socialize when the opportunity arises.

If you are having trouble keeping the puppy still without walking, then you can always do some training. Getting creative with some circuit training is a great way to tire any dog out. The training sessions you are already familiar with can be combined to make a circuit training session. You are probably familiar with dog owners that throw a ball or whatever for the dog to chase and retrieve. This again is a great way to get him racing off after the ball and then racing back again. Unfortunately though, not all dogs are immediately responsive to this and may need some initial training to get them used to the idea.

6.) Stress

a.) Short Term Stress

Stress is a biological response to a perceived threat. Biologically the dog's body is programmed to keep the animal safe by reacting in a certain way to fear. The natural reaction, at a very basic level, involves the release of very specific hormones into the dog's body which prepare the animal to deal with a threatening situation.

The subconscious preparation that happens within the body of the dog involves sending adrenaline to each of the muscles thus preparing the dog for a fight or to take flight.

In addition to this, the dog's body redirects energy to the places that will best provide immediate safety. The heart rate raises whilst digestion, immunity and reproductive organs are literally 'switched off' as each of these are secondary functions to the need for basic survival.

The dog's decision at this point will usually depend on a mixture of genetic responses and his experience of life so far. Similarly the things that a dog gets stressed about will be determined by the animal as an individual.

Some dogs, for instance, will get stressed in the car whilst others are stressed and fearful during fireworks season. Dogs that have not been properly socialized will often get stressed in the company of other dogs, simply because they don't know how to react.

B.) Long Term Stress

So now we know, in very basic terms, what an immediate stress reaction does to the dog. We will focus further on the dog's immediate reaction later but for now let's take a look at exactly what long term stress does to a dog.

Long term stress leads to dysfunction in digestion, loss of general condition and eventually many illnesses because the immune system is busy elsewhere.

C.) What Causes Stress?

This is where it gets really interesting. Stress can be caused by anything at all. This is a subject where dogs and humans are very much alike.

Just as we are all different and some of us can deal with a lot of stress before we cave in, dogs are exactly the same. Some can cope with anything at all and others deal with things by becoming stressed about them.

Common causes of stress are;

* Allergies
* Under socialization
* Lack of training
* Insufficient exercise
* An insecure environment
* Excessive noise
* Over exercise
* Agility and other sports that cause adrenaline release in the body of the dog.

Your job as the guardian and friend of a Vizsla, is to recognize any stressors in the life of your dog and make changes.

For instance, if your dog eats food with known allergens then change his food type. If your Vizsla is worried about other dogs, do some careful socialization training. If your friend is completely stressed during firework season, take some precautions to help him through it, such as Bach Flower remedy, or simply comforting him and not leaving him alone.

7.) Natural Therapy and Remedies

Natural therapy is often passed over because conventional medicine has become such a big part of our lives. This is a pity in many ways as remedies, hands on therapy and a mixture of the two can have such amazing results.

Before conventional medicine, ailments were treated with herbs, flower remedies and massage. This type of treatment healed many and let's face it conventional medicine is based upon the same approach but is far more complex.

Natural therapy is inclusive of flower remedies used for emotional balance. Herbal remedies are created from plants to support the body and immune system. Homeopathic remedies are created directly from disease at a cellular level in order to provoke immunity.

Physical therapy includes massage, hands on healing methods such as canine touch, hydrotherapy (the strengthening of muscles with the use of water) and re-alignment techniques such as canine chiropractic treatment.

All of the above have an undisputable place in the health and well-being of your Vizsla dog. So whilst the veterinarian may prescribe painkillers, a parallel natural hands-on treatment is also an option that should be considered.

As the guardian of a Vizsla it is vitally important that you do not put his health completely into the hands of someone else, not even the veterinarian. Of course in an emergency situation the vet is the most important person to turn to. However, for routine, perhaps less serious conditions you are perhaps better placed to work out what is best for him on a holistic basis.

Your veterinarian can diagnose, treat with drugs and give you advice. But it is up to you then to go away and explore all of the options available to you and your dog.

In the book ***Veterinary Secrets: Natural Health for Dogs and Cats, (2014) Dr. Andrew Jones*** talks through the place of veterinary medicine in the life of your dog and this book is a welcome addition to the care kit of any Vizsla dog. Similarly the book ***The Veterinarians Guide to Natural Remedies for Dogs (2014)*** by ***Martin Zucker,*** is also a fantastic resource for any dog owner.

Chapter Nine

Parasites, Worms and Common Illnesses

This chapter deals with the unfortunate subject of parasites and common illnesses that can affect your Vizsla. Please do not skip this chapter as it is important that you are aware of these parasites and conditions and can therefore deal with their treatment and prevention.

1.) PARASITIC WORMS

A huge concern within the digestive process are parasites.

Worms are known as internal parasites of which there are plenty that can affect the Vizsla dog and Vizsla puppies.

A.) ROUNDWORMS

The most common worm type is the roundworm, of which there are a few variations. Symptoms of a roundworm infection include itchiness in the anus area, worms in the dog's feces and loss of condition.

A mother dog can pass roundworms on to her puppies and all Vizsla puppies, bred and raised well, will be wormed properly by the breeder before sent to their new homes. Worms usually live in the dog's digestive system and some are actually symptom-less, whilst others can have serious consequences for the health of the Vizsla dog.

Hookworm and whipworm are also roundworm types that cause pain and digestive upset in dogs. The hookworm grips onto the stomach wall causing constant and severe discomfort to the dog.

A roundworm infection within the digestive system of the dog can affect general condition, though roundworm larvae has far more sinister potential.

Roundworms are a zoonotic parasite which means that they can be passed between species.

If roundworm larvae is ingested by humans it can become confused within the body and head for the eye area. The aim for the worm is to eat its way out of the retina causing blindness.

B.) TAPEWORMS

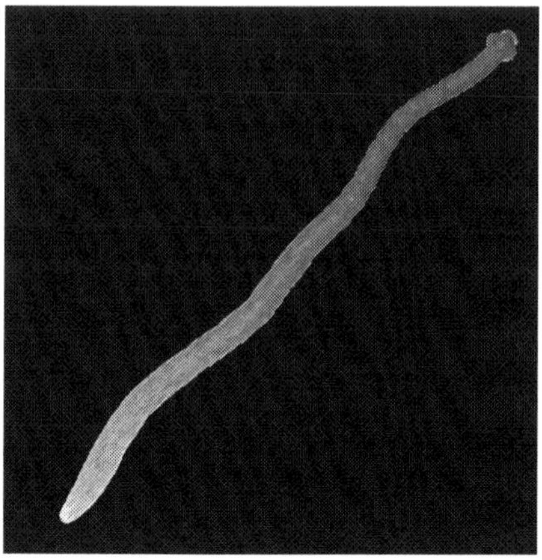

The tapeworm is a type of parasite which can sit in the intestine without doing any damage, other than consuming nutrients that your dog should be consuming. They will also grow to a large size throughout the intestinal tract. The tapeworm reproduces by shedding parts of its long and segmented body, which is passed with the feces or drops from the anus of the dog. The tapeworm is happy to live in the digestive system of both dogs and people. Again the main problem here is that it will consume a considerable amount of ingested food and obviously grow as a result. As you can imagine, your dog will not be getting sufficient nutrients and will suffer as a result.

Basic worming tablets will keep the chance of infection under control. As a routine these should be administered about every 3 months. Be careful that you are giving your dog the correct dosage. This is usually gauged by kilo weight of your dog. Also be aware that different brands suggest a different number of tablets. This is probably because of the size or potency of each tablet.

C.) LUNGWORMS/ HEARTWORMS

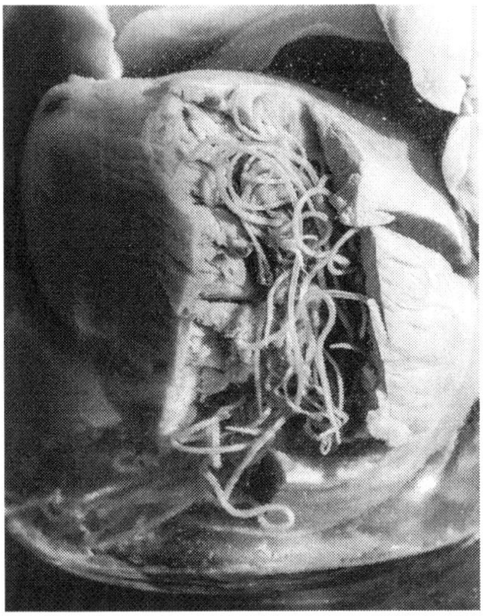

The other type of worm, and one which has serious consequences, is the lungworm/heartworm.

The larvae for this type of worm, when it gets into the body, migrates to either the lung or heart of the animal. It then quickly breeds to fill the major organ with worms, as illustrated above. By the time that the symptoms of this type of infestation appears, the damage to either the heart or lungs will be well underway.

Symptoms are excessive coughing and loss of heart or lung function. This parasite type is becoming more common, and currently being diagnosed in geographical areas where it has not previously been seen.

The larvae of this parasite enters the body via a mosquito bite or ingestion. Dogs that eat slugs, snails and their eggs are particularly susceptible to an infestation of heart or lungworm.

With quick spreading infection, has come preventative medicine. If you are in an area that is high risk, I would urge you to consult with your veterinarian about preventive measures.

As a matter of routine, you are strongly advised to check with your vet, the general type of worms your dog may be susceptible to. Worming tablets can be bought at pet stores and many general stores seem to stock these now. Once again, always make sure you choose the correct type and dosage for both your dogs size and age.

2.) EXTERNAL PARASITES – FLEAS AND OTHER SUCKERS

The other type of parasite that can potentially affect your Vizsla dog is the external parasite.

A.) FLEAS

The flea is an inventive little jumper that can hop up to half a meter and jumps onto dark areas. Therefore if your dog walks passed a flea on the ground the little insect is likely to hop on.

As soon as she finds her host the female flea will begin to lay eggs and in her lifespan of up to a month, she can easily leave up to 800 eggs on your dog and in your living environment. Eggs will wait for months, until the time and temperature is right before hatching which is why in the springtime there is a big increase in fleas.

Symptoms of fleas are grit like dirt that turns red in water and a profusion of itchy bites.

Many vets will advise that chemical treatment will need to occur every few months as a preventative measure. This is usually in the form of a spot on treatment applied to the back of the dog's neck.

Holistic veterinarians advise that a dog will only need chemical treatments in the event of an actual infestation and I'm inclined to agree with this. The logic behind this thinking is to avoid exposing the dog to a chemical substance unless it is absolutely necessary. If you find your dog is not constantly under attack in the summer months, just apply when you notice symptoms and not routinely for the sake of it.

If you keep your Vizsla healthy, well fed, clean and rinse him in a lemon juice or apple cider vinegar solution (mixed 1 part lemon/vinegar to 4 parts water) once a week, then that should keep your dog, flea free, without any need for stronger chemicals.

I also like essential oils such as cedar-wood, lemon-grass, citronella, neem and rosemary among others. There has been a lot of talk on the internet about the benefits of using these as natural flea/tick repellents. There are also some interesting videos on Youtube from people uploading their favorite remedy.

B.) TICKS

Ticks are a completely different type of parasite. They do not live on the dog but simply wander onto the animal in order to feed then drop off when full.

An empty tick looking for food (blood) is not actually much bigger than the head of a pin, and then expand in some cases to resemble a small pea. After finding a suitable spot on the body of the dog, the tick dives in by burying its tiny head under the skin and sucks as much blood as it can take, then drops off, (unlike the flea who sets up home on your dog). This is when you find them in the crate, dog bed or on the floor.

Ticks do not differentiate and will happily bite people, sheep, deer and cattle alongside dogs. They are usually only around in the summer months, but in areas of plentiful wildlife or farming environments they come in force during the warm weather, particularly when the grass gets long.

To remove a tick it is important not to squeeze its body whilst it feeds. This can cause the stomach contents and innards to be pushed into your dog's body. It is also important not to just pull as this can leave the head under the dog's skin even if you remove the body. Be careful, because if the head is left attached this can easily lead to infection. If this happens, seek veterinary attention without delay.

Pet stores sell small hooks which can be put between the tick's body and your dog's skin for careful removal, this will safely remove the parasite completely.

There is advice, mostly on the internet that suggests all sorts of cigarette burning and similar harsh approaches that aim to shock the tick into releasing its grip, all are best avoided for obvious safety reasons.

I would suggest either getting a friend or vet, who has experience of how to remove ticks to help you, or watch a step by step video from Youtube. The tick attaches itself in a spiral clockwise direction. So with tweezers or one of the specially designed hooks to grip the body of the tick you then gently twist in an anti-clockwise direction. This effectively unhooks the tick and avoids you accidentally twisting the head off.

You may wonder, if the tick eventually drops off anyway why go to all this trouble of removing it. Well the main concern with ticks is that in some geographical areas they carry Lyme disease which will most certainly need veterinary and medical attention. Symptoms of the disease are fatigue, muscle pain and joint problems. People alongside dogs are susceptible to Lyme disease if bitten by a host tick.

C.) Mites

Mites are everywhere. Generally they do us no harm, yet some can cause problems for the Vizsla dog, particularly the mange mite.

Mange mites burrow under the skin of the dog and cause itchiness and general hair loss. Left untreated the mange mite will affect the general health of the animal and result in eventual baldness.

The immune system of the dog is severely affected by the presence of mange mites. If not treated, the seemingly simple mange infestation will be fatal.

Any dog that is suspected of carrying mange mites should be treated by conventional veterinary medicine. The condition can be really difficult to get rid of and the course of treatment may be long and slow.

If your Vizsla is itchy in the autumn time, then he may be suffering with a reaction to harvest mites, particularly if you live on farmland. Other than irritation, these little mites are harmless and can be washed away with soap and water.

D.) Ear Mites

Ear mites cannot be seen by the human eye but are easily visible with the use of a microscope. These little mites grow and reproduce in the dog's ear and create a very smelly brown discharge. Ear mites are usually easily treated with drops.

E.) Flies

Flies in the summer are a real hazard if your dog has any open wounds or sores. The big flies are continually looking for somewhere to lay eggs, which quickly grow into maggots and eat their way beneath the flesh. This is a condition called 'fly strike' which often affects pet rabbits and similar animals.

So if your dog has anything from a small flesh wound to sore anal glands ensure that the heat does not leave him vulnerable to this particular nasty parasite.

3.) OTHER COMMON ILLNESSES

Vizsla health is something that every owner of the breed should be aware of. Dogs get sick sometimes, they have off days, and they are susceptible to passing bugs, just as we are.

To have a basic understanding of the way that these things affect the body of your dog, will put you in the best position to help him.

A.) DIARRHEA

Diarrhea is a common occurrence and not normally one to worry too much about.

If the Vizsla dog does display symptoms you can simply withhold his food for 24 hours then re-introduce it gradually.

If the following symptoms occur, then it is important to visit your veterinary surgeon as soon as possible;

* The condition does not clear up within a few days

* The dog is passing blood

* The dog has eaten something potentially toxic such as chocolate or artificial sweetener

* The dog is lethargic or staggering

* The dog's gums are very pale or very dark red

* When pinched, the back of the dogs neck does not spring back into place – this is a sign of dehydration

B.) VOMITING

Dogs vomit by choice, so a one off incident is usually nothing much to worry about. You will see them eating grass for instance, and then sometime later you may notice a pile of chewed up grass and mucous/stomach contents. Although eating grass doesn't always lead a dog to vomit, it may be one of the reasons you may see them vomit. It is generally thought they may vomit if they feel ill and need to empty their stomach, much the same as we may need to vomit and then feel much better afterwards.

Yet if the following circumstances are associated with vomiting, then the dog should be taken along to the veterinarian;

* The dog has not long been chewing a bone or toy that could possibly be stuck in his digestive system.

* The dog could have been exposed to poisons.

* The dog's airway is obstructed either alongside or as a result of vomiting.

If either of the previous conditions are worrying you to excess, or seem too severe to ignore, even if your concern is caused by an instinctive 'gut' feeling; this should result in a check-up with the vet.

You know your dog better than anyone else. If you are overly worried, then it is a good idea to listen to those concerns. Your Vizsla dog's health may depend on your instinct at some point in your lives together.

Chapter Ten:

Keeping Your Vizsla Healthy

Even if you give your dog a healthy diet and a safe environment, he may still be prone to developing certain health problems. Familiarizing yourself with the health problems to which this breed is prone will help you to identify them early on so you can provide your dog with the necessary treatment. In this chapter you will find valuable information about Vizsla diseases, vaccination schedules and information, nutritional deficiencies, and pet insurance.

1.) Common Vizsla Health Problems

All dogs are prone to developing certain diseases, and congenital conditions can be passed from the parent dogs to the puppies. In this section you will find an overview of the various diseases to which the smooth and wire-coated Vizsla are prone so you can prepare yourself in the event that your Vizsla comes down with something.

The following diseases and disorders are common to the Vizsla breed:

Important!

* Atopic Dermatitis
* Epilepsy
* Entropion/Ectropion
* Gastric Torsion
* Hemangiosarcoma
* Hip Dysplasia
* Hypothyroidism
* Lymphoma
* Polymyositis
* Sebaceous Adenitis

In the following pages you will receive an overview of each of these ten diseases including information about causes, symptoms, and treatments. The more you know about these diseases the better equipped you will be to handle them if they occur. The earlier your Vizsla receives a diagnosis, the more effective the treatment will be, and the greater his chances of making a full recovery.

a.) Atopic Dermatitis

Atopic dermatitis is simply another name for skin allergies in Vizslas. The condition of your dog's skin is like a window to his inner health. If your dog doesn't appear healthy on the outside, there is probably something wrong on the inside. Some of the most common signs of skin allergies and other skin problems include hair loss, scratching, frequent licking, rubbing the body on objects, rashes, blisters, hot spots, and lesions. Your dog may also exhibit internal symptoms that manifest externally such as diarrhea or vomiting caused by certain allergies.

Like humans, dogs can be allergic to a wide variety of things including pollen, dust, mold, dander, cigarette smoke, fleas/flea products, perfumes, fabrics, and certain food ingredients. To diagnose skin allergies and other problems, your veterinarian may perform a variety of diagnostic tests. The only way to test for a food allergy, however, is to switch to an allergen-free dog food formula for 10 to 12 weeks and then to systematically introduce potential allergens to test your dog's reaction. Once you have determined the cause of the allergy you can take steps to remove it from your dog's diet.

Certain types of allergies cannot be treated by removing them from your dog's life. For example, you cannot completely prevent your dog from coming into contact with pollen or dust. Certain medications may help to manage your dog's allergy symptoms. Antihistamines like Benadryl, for example, may benefit certain dogs and supplements of fatty acids might help to improve your dog's skin and coat condition. If your dog's allergies are very severe he may require treatment with a corticosteroid medication. These medications require close monitoring by your veterinarian.

B) Vizsla Allergies

Dog allergies can be problematic and any dog can be prone to or become allergic to anything from the dust in the home to grains in his diet.

Wheat Allergies

Wheat and grain allergy can cause so many health problems that grain free dog food is actually becoming quite a common product and many pet stores have at least one available variety, if not multiple types.

What is wheat allergy though, and what problems can it cause Vizsla dogs and their puppies

Wheat related health problems in dogs are actually split into three different reactions; wheat allergy, gluten allergy and gluten intolerance. Each has a slightly different reaction on the body, all with equal detriment.

In short, wheat in a dog's diet can lead to a number of different allergy related symptoms of varying severity. Take a look;

Be Aware!

* Itchy skin
* Open sores
* Ear infections
* Breathing problems
* Hives
* Itching of the mouth or throat
* Itchy and watery eyes
* Itchiness
* Dry skin
* Lack of coat condition and dandruff
* Loose bowel movements
* Nasal congestion
* Rash
* Skin swelling
* Vomiting

Gluten sensitivity is a reaction specific to gluten, found within wheat, symptoms include;

Be Aware!

* Changes in behavior
* Bone and joint discomfort
* Pain
* Muscle cramps
* Weight loss
* Fatigue

The biology behind allergic reactions, in very simple terms, is that allergy attacks the immune system of the dog.

When the dog is eating a diet high in something that he is allergic to, the body has to constantly fight the introduction of the substance in the body. This leaves the dog's immune system weakened and less able to cope with other infections and illnesses.

Although wheat is one of the major factors in dog food allergy, there are many more. Ingredients in dog food range vastly dependent on the brand but they can include bright colors (to appeal to you, the dog owner) unnatural flavors and shocking chemical preservatives.

Take a look at your favorite dog food for a moment, or spend some time in the aisles of the pet store, the composition of most dog food is pretty terrifying. Long chemical names and a huge list of them are worrying to say the least.

C.) EPILEPSY

Canine epilepsy is a very serious condition known to affect the Vizsla breed. This condition is the most common neurological condition seen in dogs and it can affect as much as 5% of the canine population. Epilepsy is not actually a single disease. A diagnosis of epilepsy generally refers to any of a number of conditions characterized by recurring seizures. Seizure conditions in dogs can be genetically inherited, caused by anatomical abnormalities in the brain, or they may stem from an unknown cause in some cases.

There is a widely-accepted classification system for seizures in humans but one has not yet been adopted for dogs. There are several different types of seizures such as those that involve involuntary muscle movements or motor seizures which affect localized areas. An automatism is a type of motor seizure which often looks like a voluntary behavior like chewing or barking. Non-motor seizures do happen in dogs but they are more difficult to detect as they often involve the perception of a sensory stimulus that isn't actually present. You may therefore observe the dog biting at nonexistent flies or staring off into space.

Unfortunately, there is no cure for canine epilepsy but there are a variety of treatment options available to help control the disease. Anti-epileptic drugs like potassium bromide, phenobarbital, and felbamate are commonly administered to reduce seizure activity. Research is still being conducted regarding the causes of canine epilepsy, both inherited and acquired, in order to make treatment options more effective.

d.) Entropion/Ectropion

Vizslas are prone to developing several eye problems but the most common are entropion and ectropion. Entropion is a genetic condition in which part of the eyelid becomes folded or inverted. Ectropion occurs when the lower lid turns outward, leaving the inner eyelid exposed and prone to irritation. The most commonly seen form of ectropion in Vizslas is inherited, though it can also be caused by hypothyroidism, facial nerve paralysis, scarring, or chronic inflammation of tissues around the eye. Entropion is also inherited in many cases, though repeated eye infections or trauma to the eye can contribute to development of the disease as well.

Diagnosis of entropion is fairly straightforward because it causes visible irritation to the surface of the eye and often causes inflammation of the surrounding tissue. In most cases, the secondary problems caused by entropion are addressed first. In mild cases, treatment for corneal scratches may consist of lubrication with artificial tears. In moderate to severe cases, surgery may be required to correct the malformation and to prevent it from recurring. Follow-up care and medications may be required after surgical treatments.

Ectropion is also diagnosed through physical examination, though additional blood and urine tests may be performed to diagnose the underlying cause of the problem. Mild ectropion is usually treated with medical therapy like lubricating eye drops or ointments to prevent the eye from drying out. In severe cases, surgery may be the only corrective option. The prognosis for surgical correction is usually very good, though some cases will require two or more surgeries to permanently correct the issue.

e.) Gastric Torsion

Also known as bloat, gastric torsion is a condition that commonly affects large-breed dogs though it has been known to happen in the Vizsla as well. This condition occurs when the dog's stomach dilates (swells) and then it rotates on its short axis. This torsion can result in a number of serious conditions such as pressure within the abdomen, progressive distension of the stomach, and damage to the cardiovascular system. Decreased perfusion may also occur which could lead to damage to the body's cells and a potential for organ failure.

The symptoms of gastric torsion often include depression, anxiety, abdominal pain, distention of the stomach, collapse, excessive drooling, vomiting and dry heaving. As the condition progresses the dog may also experience an increased heart rate, a weak pulse, and labored breathing. The causes of this condition are largely unknown, unfortunately though, dogs that have a parent or other relative who have experienced the disease, are at a higher risk. Deep-chested breeds are also at an increased risk for gastric torsion.

Because gastric torsion can quickly escalate and lead to emergency conditions, it is essential that you seek treatment for your Vizsla as soon as you suspect the condition. Hospitalization is generally required, especially if your dog is experiencing cardiovascular symptoms. Once the heart problems have been treated, the pressure in the abdomen will be released through orogastric intubation. After this happens, surgery may be performed to correct the position of the stomach. Additional treatments may be required in some cases to correct additional organ damage.

F.) Hemangiosarcoma

Hemangiosarcoma is a type of very aggressive, malignant tumor which affects the blood vessels that line the cells. The most common location for hemangiosarcoma tumors is in the spleen, though they can technically occur anywhere there are blood vessels in the body. Other locations that may be affected include the liver, heart, bone, and skin. Hemangiosarcoma tumors are divided into three classifications – dermal, hypodermal or subcutaneous, and visceral.

A tumor caused by hemangiosarcoma may produce a variety of symptoms including a lump under the skin, visible bleeding, abdominal swelling, or pale color in the gums. This condition may also result in behavioral changes like unexplained weakness, collapse, depression, seizures, and difficulty breathing. Unfortunately, this condition typically affects the internal organs so many dogs do not show outward symptoms until the disease has progressed to the severest form.

Hemangiosarcoma is known to affect a number of different breeds and it most commonly develops in dogs aged 6 to 13 years. Diagnosis of hemangiosarcoma will require a thorough examination as well as diagnostic tests including blood counts, chemistry panels, urinalysis and x-rays. To make a definitive diagnosis, a biopsy of the tumor will also be taken. Treatment varies depending on the location of the tumor and its size at diagnosis. Treatment options are most successful when the tumor is in the skin and many small dermal tumors can be treated through surgical removal. More severe tumors and those affecting the internal organs may require chemotherapy and/or radiation therapy.

G.) Hip Dysplasia

Hip dysplasia is a musculoskeletal issue seen in many dogs but it is particularly common in large and medium-sized breeds. This condition is characterized by a malformation of the hip joint which causes the femur to pop in and out of the socket, causing painful wear and tear and osteoarthritis. Most dogs that suffer from this condition are born with normal hips but various factors result in the soft tissues around the hip developing in an abnormal way which then affects the joint itself.

This condition affects dogs of all ages. In severe cases, puppies just a few months old may begin showing signs of pain or discomfort related to hip dysplasia. These symptoms are most likely to occur during and after exercise, and the condition may worsen to the point that normal daily activity becomes painful. If the dog does not receive treatment, the condition will progress to the point that the dog becomes lame and unable to walk. In most cases, symptoms of hip dysplasia do not develop until middle age or in the later years of life.

The most common symptoms of hip dysplasia in Vizslas and other breeds are closely linked to the symptoms of arthritis. Most dogs will exhibit an altered gait while walking or running and some resist movement that requires them to fully extend or flex their back legs. Some dogs may move with a bunny hop-like gait and they may have trouble navigating stairs. Dogs with hip dysplasia are often very sore or stiff when they get up in the morning and when they rise from lying down for a period of time. Over time, dogs affected by this condition may become more lethargic and less willing to play.

Hip dysplasia is primarily an inherited condition, so you may not be able to prevent your Vizsla from developing it if he has a genetic predisposition. Certain medical treatments like dietary changes, anti-inflammatory medications, and supplements may help your dog to deal with the pain and they might slow the progression of the disease. The most permanent and effective treatments, however, are surgical. Surgery can be performed to re-align the bones and joints or to completely replace the hip. Surgery can also be done to remove the femoral head and to replace it with a pseudo-joint. This is the surgical treatment most commonly used.

H.) HYPOTHYROIDISM

This condition is caused by a deficiency in thyroid hormones. The thyroid is an essential gland in the body which produces a variety of different hormones that play a role in your dog's metabolism. Reduced production of T3 and T4 hormones (liothyronine and levothyroxine) results in hypothyroidism. This condition is most common in small and medium-sized breeds; with certain breeds having a greater predisposition than others. This condition most commonly affects dogs between 4 and 10 years of age, and spayed/neutered dogs are more at-risk for hypothyroidism than intact dogs.

Some of the most common symptoms of hypothyroidism include lethargy, weakness, mental dullness, unexplained weight gain, hair loss, poor hair growth, scaling, recurring skin infections, intolerance to cold and seizures. Hypothyroidism can be caused by several different things including iodine deficiency, cancer, and heredity. It can also be an after-effect of certain medical treatments like surgery. Extensive testing may be required to diagnose this condition and to determine its cause, and therefore the course of treatment.

Treatment for hypothyroidism typically involves medication and some form of dietary modification. Medical treatments involve synthetic hormone supplements or other medications. Dietary modifications recommended for hypothyroidism include a low-fat diet, especially during the initial phase of therapy. Most dogs respond to treatment for this condition within a few weeks.

I.) LYMPHOMA

Lymphoma is fairly rare in dogs but it has been seen in the Vizsla breed. This condition is a type of cancer that begins in the lymphocyte cells which are part of the immune system. Lymphocytes are a type of white blood cell and there are two different kinds – T cells and B cells. Most cases of lymphoma seen in dogs affect the B-lymphocytes.

The symptoms of lymphoma in dogs may vary depending on the severity of the condition as well as the location of the tumor. Generally, symptoms include loss of appetite, lethargy, weakness, and weight loss. The exact cause of lymphoma is largely unknown and diagnosis of this condition can be difficult. A thorough examination will be required in addition to blood tests and urinalysis.

Unfortunately, there is no cure for lymphoma in dogs and many dogs relapse after treatment. The most common treatments are chemotherapy and radiation therapy. Fluid therapy may also be recommended for cases that involve dehydration. Some cases of lymphoma never improve and in most cases the goal of treatment is simply to improve the quality of the dog's life.

J.) Polymyositis

Polymyositis is a type of immune-mediated disease affecting the skeletal muscle of dogs. This condition can affect any type of skeletal muscle including those in the limbs, the esophagus, or the mouth. This condition can occur on its own or in conjunction with other immune-mediated diseases like systemic lupus. Breed-specific polymyositis has been reported in just a few breeds, including the Hungarian Vizsla.

This condition most commonly affects middle-aged dogs and the common symptoms are weakness, stiffened gait, weight loss, vomiting, muscle atrophy, and contractures to skeletal muscles. The most common causes of polymyositis in Vizslas include cancer, immune-mediated infections, and reaction to certain drugs. Diagnosis will require a thorough medical history and examination as well as blood count, urinalysis and thoracic x-rays in some cases.

The most common treatment for polymyositis in Vizslas are corticosteroids to suppress the immune system overreaction. In many cases, this is the underlying cause of the condition. In some cases, antibiotics may also be prescribed to help fight off infection. In addition to medical treatments you may also need to increase your pet's physical activity in order to strengthen his muscles and to stave off atrophy. Dogs having an enlarged esophagus may require special feeding techniques. Your veterinarian will be able to tell you more about how your dog should be fed and what types of food you should offer.

K.) Sebaceaous Adenitis

Also known as inflammatory skin disease; sebaceous adenitis in dogs is a fairly rare condition. This disease typically affects the skin glands of young and middle-aged dogs. There are two different types of sebaceous adenitis; one that occurs in long-coated breeds and the other in short-coated. The short-coated variety is the type that affects the Vizsla.

Common symptoms of sebaceous adenitis in long-coated dogs include alopecia (hair loss), odor along the hairline, clumps of matted hair, dull or brittle hair, intense itching, bacterial skin infections, and skin lesions. In short-coated breeds, the most common symptoms are alopecia (often in a circular pattern), mild scaling of the skin on the head and trunk, and secondary bacterial infections along the hairline. The cause for this condition remains unidentified, though researchers are working on it.

The most common diagnostic procedures used for this disease include skin scrapings and endocrine function tests. A skin biopsy may also be required in certain cases as well as pathologic testing of the sebaceous glands. Treatment for this condition varies depending on the severity and the type of sebaceous adenitis. Some of the most common treatments include brushing to remove flaking, internal medication, antibacterial products, soaking and massaging the skin in oil, and various shampoos or skin rubs to reduce itching.

2.) Preventing Illness – Vaccinations

Though you may not be able to prevent your Vizsla from developing certain inherited conditions if he already has a genetic predisposition, there are certain diseases you can prevent with vaccinations. During the first few weeks of life, your Vizsla puppy relies on the antibodies he receives from his mother's milk to fend off infection and illness. Once his own immune system develops, however, you will be able to administer vaccines to prevent certain diseases like canine distemper, parvovirus, and rabies.

Vaccinations for dogs can be divided into two categories: core vaccines, and non-core vaccines. Core vaccines are those that every dog should receive while non-core vaccines are administered based on your dog's level of risk. Depending on where you live and how often your Vizsla comes into contact with other dogs, you may not need to administer any non-core vaccines. According to the AVMA, recommended core vaccines for dogs include: distemper, canine adenovirus, canine parvovirus, and rabies. Non-core vaccines include: coronavirus, leptospirosis,

Bordetella bronchiseptica, canine parainfluenza, and Borrelia burgdorferi. You will need to speak to your veterinarian about non-core vaccines to determine which ones your Vizsla does and doesn't need. The rabies vaccine can be very stressful for dogs but, unfortunately, it is necessary in the United States due to the prevalence of rabies in wild animals. Rabies has been eradicated in the U.K. so dogs living in this area will not need rabies vaccines. Some veterinarians recommend that you only administer the rabies vaccine every three years. However, some states require an annual rabies vaccine, so be sure to check with your local council.

It is important to note however that a rabies vaccine should not be administered less than one month before or after a combination vaccine.

The Vizsla that will be going into kennels may need to be immunized against canine kennel cough too. Most boarding establishments insist on it.

Kennel cough immunization is via drops squirted up the dog's nose. It can be quite a stressful experience for dog and owner.

After the initial vaccination has been given, this is where the need for boosters becomes hazy. Some veterinarians state that a dog must get a booster every year whilst others think that it is a needless assault on the dog's immune system leaving the animal susceptible to illness.

Although the yearly booster and associated parasite prevention chemicals are standard procedure, at present more veterinarians are questioning the need for it.

This is because each of the treatments has an effect on the dog's immune system and may leave the dog susceptible to passing viruses, illnesses which grow within the body, or bacteria in the environment.

Your veterinarian will be able to provide you with specific vaccination recommendations for your Vizsla but, for reference, you will find a general vaccination schedule for dogs below:

Recommended Vaccination Schedule

Vaccine	*Doses*	*Age*	*Booster*
Rabies	*1*	*12 weeks*	*Annually*
Distemper	*3*	*6 to 16 weeks*	*3 Years*
Parvovirus	*3*	*6 to 16 weeks*	*3 Years*
Adenovirus	*3*	*6 to 16 weeks*	*3 Years*
Parainfluenza	*3*	*6 weeks, 12 to 14 weeks*	*3 Years*
Bordetella	*1*	*6 weeks*	*Annually*
Lyme Disease	*2*	*9, 13 to 14 weeks*	*Annually*
Leptospirosis	*2*	*12 and 16 weeks*	*Annually*
Canine Influenza	*2*	*6 to 8; 8 to 12 weeks*	*Annually*

Please note: **Titre testing** is commonly practised to establish whether a dog that has been immunized, is in need of a booster for a specific vaccine. This is carried out by a simple laboratory blood test. If sufficient antibodies are present, then there is no need to vaccinate with that specific vaccine. Once again, please note that regular, unnecessary vaccinating, can have an adverse affect on your dogs health. It would also constitute a waste of money.

3.) PET INSURANCE – DO YOU NEED IT

Many new dog owners wonder whether pet insurance is a good option or whether it is a waste of money. The truth of the matter is that it is different in different cases. Pet insurance does for your pet what health insurance does for you; it helps to mitigate your out-of-pocket costs by providing coverage for certain services. While health insurance-for humans covers all kinds of health-care including preventive care, disease treatment, and accident coverage, pet insurance is a little more limited. Some pet insurance plans only cover accidents while others cover illnesses. Some plans cover certain preventive care options like spay/neuter surgery or vaccinations, but generally only during a puppy's first year.

The costs for pet insurance plans vary from one company to another and from one plan to another.

Pet insurance works in a very different way than health insurance when it comes to payment. With a health insurance plan you might be asked to pay a co-payment to your doctor when you visit his office but the health plan will

forward the remaining payment directly to the provider. With a pet insurance plan you will be required to pay for the treatment up-front and then submit a claim to receive reimbursement for costs up to 90%. The actual amount a pet insurance plan will cover, varies from one plan to another and it may depend on the deductible amount you select as well.

Just as you would with a health insurance plan, having a pet insurance plan requires you to pay a monthly premium. As long as you remain current with those payments however, you are eligible to receive benefits from the plan. Keep in mind though, that most pet insurance plans have some kind of deductible in place. A deductible is a set amount that you must pay out-of-pocket before the plan will offer reimbursement for covered services. In many cases, pet insurance plans are useful only for large expenses like cancer treatments that you normally might not be able to cover at a moment's notice. It is not, however, generally cost-effective for things like annual vet exams and vaccinations.

Estimated Cost for Pet Insurance Plans

Pet Wellness Plan	*Injury Plan (Emergency)*	*Medical Plan (Economical)*	*Major Medical Plan*
$18 to $34 per month (£11.70 to £22.10)	*$10 per month(£6.50 p/m)*	*$19 to $27 per month (£12.35 to £17.55)*	*$25 to $35 per month (£16.25 to £22.75)*
Wellness exams, Vaccinations, dental cleaning	*Injuries only (such as Poisoning and broken bones)*	*Basic coverage for accidents, emergencies and illness*	*Double benefits of Medical Plan*
3 levels (Max, plus basic)	*Max yearly benefit limit $14,000 (£9,100)*	*Max yearly benefit limit $7,000 (£4,500)*	*Max yearly benefit limit $14,000 (£9,100)*

**This information is taken from Veterinary Pet Insurance, a division of Nationwide Insurance. Prices are subject to change and are only intended to give a general idea of pricing and coverage options for pet insurance plans.

Chapter Eleven:

Showing Your Vizsla Dog

Showing your Vizsla is a great way to build your relationship with your dog and it can be an enjoyable challenge. In order for your Vizsla to do well in conformation he must meet certain breed standard requirements set forth by the AKC, the UK Kennel Club, or whatever breed governing body that is sponsoring the show. In this chapter you will learn about Vizsla breed standards and tips for showing your dog.

1.) VIZSLA BREED STANDARDS

The breed standard is simply a list of characteristics, the ideal specimen of a particular breed should embody. Breed standards are published by breed governing bodies like the American Kennel Club and the UK Kennel Club. Breed clubs like the Vizsla Club of America may also have their own version of a breed standard. If you plan to show your Vizsla you will need to become very familiar with the breed standard because it is the list of characteristics against which he will be judged. You will find a summary of the AKC Vizsla breed standard below:

General Appearance

The general appearance for the Vizsla is that of a medium-sized, short-coated breed with a distinguished hunting dog appearance and bearing. The dog is robust but lightly built; agile and energetic; with a brawny or sinewy muscular condition.

Temperament

The Vizsla is a natural hunter with a good nose and above-average train-ability. The dog is lively but well-mannered and demonstrably affectionate. Shyness and timidity should be penalized.

Head and Skull

The head is lean and muscular, the skull moderately wide between the ears with a median line down the forehead. The ears are thin and silky, the muzzle square and deep.

Legs and Body

The body is strong and well-proportioned with high withers. Proportions should be balanced with a moderately broad/deep chest and well-sprung ribs.

Tail and Coat

The coat is short, smooth, dense and close-lying – no woolly undercoat. The tail is set just below the level of the croup and docked one-third off.

Color

The coat color should be golden rust in varying shades; saddle markings are common. Pale yellow or solid dark mahogany colorations are faulty.

Size

The ideal male is 22 to 24 inches high and the ideal female is 21 to 23 inches high. Disqualifications for males over 25 ½ or under 20 ½ and females over 24 ½ or under 19 ½ inches.

Faults

Disqualifications include: partially or completely black nose; solid white extending above the toes or anywhere except the fore-chest; distinctly long coat

2.) What to Know Before You Show

If you plan to show your Vizsla dog, there are a few things you need to know before you register. The exact rules and requirements will vary from one show to another, so pay attention to specific requirements.

Before you attempt to show your Vizsla, make sure your dog meets the following general requirements:

Required!

* Your dog needs to be fully house-trained, and able to hold his bladder for several hours.

* Your Vizsla needs to be properly socialized, and able to get along well with both humans and other dogs.

* Your dog should have basic obedience training, and he should respond consistently to your commands and look to you for leadership.

* Your Vizsla should be even-tempered, not aggressive or hyperactive in public settings.

* Your dog needs to meet the specific eligibility requirements of whatever show you are participating in. There may be certain requirements for age, for example.

* Your Vizsla needs to be completely up to date on his vaccinations so there is no risk of him contracting or spreading disease among other dogs at the show.

In addition to considering these requirements, you also need to make sure that you yourself are prepared for the show.

The list on the next page will help you to know what to bring with you on the day of the show:

Advisable!

* Your dog's registration information

* A dog crate and exercise pen

* Food and water bowls for your dog

* Your dog's food and treats

* Grooming supplies and grooming table

* Trash bags for cleanup

* Any medications your dog needs

* A change of clothes for yourself

* Food and water for yourself

3.) Preparing Your Dog for Show

Your preparations for the dog show will vary according to the type of show in which you have entered. If you enter an obedience show for example, perfecting your dog's appearance may be less important than it would for a conformation show. Before you even enter your dog into a show you should consider attending a few dog shows yourself to get a feel for it. Walk around the tent where the dogs are being prepared for show and pay close attention during the judging to learn what the judges are looking for in any given show. The more you learn before you show your own dog, the better off you will be.

One of the most important things you need to do in preparation for a conformation show is to have your Vizsla properly groomed so that his coat is in good condition.

Follow the steps below to groom your Vizsla in preparation for show:

1. The night before, give your Vizsla a thorough brushing then trim his nails and clean his ears.

2. Give your dog a bath and dry his coat thoroughly before brushing him again.

3. Once your dog is clean, you need to keep him that way. Have him sleep in a crate that night and keep him on the leash during his morning walk.

4. The day of the show, brush your Vizsla's coat again.

5. When you arrive at the show, keep your dog in his crate or in a fenced exercise pen so he doesn't get dirty.

When it comes time for judging, just remember that the main reason you are doing this is to have fun with your dog. Do not get too upset if your Vizsla does not win. Just take notes of ways you can improve for the next show and enjoy the experience you and your dog had together that day.

Chapter Twelve:

Breeding Vizsla Dogs

Breeding can put a strain on your dog, especially for females; and there is always the risk for complications. You should only breed your Vizsla if you thoroughly prepare yourself through in-depth research. Additionally you need to be able to provide the care that a pregnant Vizsla and a litter of puppies will require. In this chapter you will find detailed information about Vizsla breeding to help you decide whether it is something you want to pursue.

1.) Basic Breeding Information

If you are considering breeding your Vizsla, think long and hard about your motivation for doing so. Many dog owners mistakenly believe that breeding their dog is a good way to make some extra money. In reality, by the time you cover the vet bills and other costs to care for a pregnant dog and a litter of puppies, you will be lucky to break even. If you do not plan to breed your Vizsla you should have him or her neutered or spayed before the age of 6 months. For female dogs, it is best to perform spay surgery before the dog's first heat. According to the ASPCA, spaying a female dog before her first heat can significantly reduce your dog's risk for developing mammary cancer as well as ovarian and uterine cancers.

Aside from this information, you will also find it useful to know some other facts about dog breeding in general. For example, the estrus cycle (also known as "heat") for dogs occurs twice a year – about every 6 months. This cycle typically lasts for 14 to 21 days with the length varying from one dog to another. It can take a few years for an adult dog's cycle to become regular. Many Vizsla breeders have found that their females go into heat every 6 months like clockwork; so you may be able to predict your Vizsla's cycle fairly accurately. Heat does not occur in any particular season, it is simply a matter of the dog's age and when she reaches breeding age.

If you plan to breed your Vizsla, it will be important for you to recognize the signs of estrus. The first sign that your dog is going into heat will be the swelling of the external vulva. In some cases, your dog may excrete a bloody discharge early on but this typically does not develop until the 7th day of the cycle. As your dog's cycle progresses, the discharge will become lighter in color and more watery. By the 10th day of her cycle, the discharge will be pinkish in color.

In addition to swelling of the vulva and a bloody discharge, many female Vizslas in heat will start to urinate more often than usual. Sometimes the dog will develop marking behavior, spraying urine on various objects in the home to mark her territory and to attract male dogs. A male dog can smell a female in heat from great distances, so it is very important that you keep your female Vizsla indoors when she is in heat. When you take her outside, supervise her closely and never take her to a dog park or anywhere that intact male dogs may be present.

Ovulation typically occurs at the time of your dog's cycle when the vaginal discharge becomes watery. During ovulation is when your Vizsla will be most fertile and, if you intend to breed her, this is when you should introduce her to the male dog. Your Vizsla may not be receptive to the advances of a male dog until this point in her cycle, though she is capable of becoming pregnant at any point during estrus because sperm can survive for up to 7 days in the female's reproductive tract. If your female Vizsla accidentally mates with the wrong dog you can take her to the veterinarian for a mis-mating injection. Be aware, however, that there are risks associated with this injection so discuss it carefully with your vet.

The number of puppies your Vizsla carries may vary but the average litter size for Vizslas is between 6 and 8 puppies. In most cases, new mothers will have smaller litters at first and then may carry more puppies until about her fourth litter when the number tapers off again. Once your Vizsla becomes pregnant, she will enter into a gestation period lasting about 63 days (9 weeks). You will not be able to detect your dog's pregnancy until she is about 3 weeks in, however.

Do not attempt to feel for the fetuses on your own because you could hurt your dog or the developing fetuses. An experienced veterinarian will be able to palpate your dog's uterus around day 28 to 32 of her pregnancy to confirm that she is indeed pregnant. It is safe to perform an ultrasound on a pregnant dog after 25 days, and by six weeks, pregnancy can be confirmed using x-rays.

There are also testing kits that you can buy, similar to human pregnancy testing kits. I have never personally used one, so cannot comment on how useful or accurate they are. By all means, do some research on these. I believe these are available at most pet stores.

2.) The Breeding Process

Most breeders do not recommend breeding Vizslas until they are one year old, and definitely not during the first cycle. This will give a little bit of time to get used to your dog's cycle. You will start to recognize the signs of heat in your dog and will be able to take precautions against accidental pregnancies. An intact male dog can smell a female in heat from distances up to 3 miles (4.83 km) so do not think that just because your neighbors do not have a dog that your female will be safe.

Once your dogs are of proper breeding age, you can start to think about breeding. You will need to keep a record of your female dog's estrus cycle so you will know when she is most fertile; around days 11 to 15 of the cycle. During this time is when your female dog will be most receptive to breeding. So, that is when you should introduce her to the male dog. Mating behavior may vary from one breed to another but, for the most part, you can expect the male dog to mount the female from behind. The male will ejaculate his sperm into the female's reproductive tract where it will fertilize the eggs. If the eggs are fertilized, conception occurs and the female becomes pregnant and enters into the gestation period which, as previously noted, lasts about 59 to 63 days.

You must keep track of when you breed your female dog so you will know when to expect her to whelp the puppies (give birth). Once again, by the third week of pregnancy, around day 21, your veterinarian will be able to confirm whether the dog is pregnant or not. He may also be able to give you an estimate as to her litter size. Treat your pregnant female as you normally would until the fourth or fifth week of pregnancy, then you should start to increase her feeding rations proportionally with her weight gain. This has been covered in the chapter on feeding and calorie needs, so please refer back to that. You only need to increase your dog's diet slightly to account for her increased nutritional needs. Having said that, your dog will know how much she needs to eat, so you may be able to let her feed freely rather than rationing her food.

It is also around this time that your Vizsla will start to look visibly pregnant. Your dog's belly will grow larger, tighter, and harder and her nipples will become especially swollen during the last week of pregnancy. Your pregnant dog's diet should be high in protein and animal fat with plenty of calcium.

3.) Raising Vizsla Puppies

By the eighth week of your dog's pregnancy you will need to provide her with a whelping box. This should be a comfortable place lined with old clean blankets and towels where she can give birth and care for the puppies. It is best to place this box in a quiet area where your dog will not be disturbed. If you put it somewhere that is too bright or noisy, she will just find somewhere else to whelp.

During the last week of your Vizsla's pregnancy you should start checking her internal temperature regularly. The normal body temperature for a dog is between 100°F and 102°F (37.7°C to 38.8°C). Your female dog's body temperature will drop, however, about 24 hours before contractions begin. Your dog's body temperature may drop as low as 98°F (36.6°C), so when you notice a drop in your dog's temperature you can be sure that it won't be long before the puppies arrive. Your dog will also start spending more time in the whelping box at this time. You can check on her occasionally, but do not disturb her too much or she might go elsewhere to whelp.

When your Vizsla goes into labor, you will notice obvious signs of discomfort. She may start pacing restlessly and panting, switching from one position to another without seeming to get comfortable. The early stages of labor can last for several hours with contractions occurring about 10 minutes apart. This usually occurs in waves of 3 to 5 contractions followed by a period of rest. If your Vizsla has two hours of contractions without any puppies being born, take her to the vet immediately. Without a veterinary diagnosis, it is difficult to ascertain what the problem may be, but as with human pregnancies, she may need a caesarian section.

Once your Vizsla starts whelping, the puppies will generally arrive every thirty minutes, following ten to thirty minutes of forceful straining from the female. When a puppy is born, the mother will clean the puppy and bite off the umbilical cord. Not only does licking clean the puppy, but it helps to stimulate its breathing as well. You need to let the mother do this without you attempting to handle the puppies unless something goes wrong. After all of the puppies have been whelped, the female will expel the rest of the placenta and then allow the puppies to nurse (feed). The bitch may attempt to eat the placenta, which is normal.

It is very important that the puppies start nursing (feeding) within 1 hour of delivery because this is when they will get the colostrum. The colostrum is the first milk produced by the mother and it is loaded not only with vitamins and minerals, but it contains antibodies as well, that will protect the puppies against illness and infection while their own immune systems are developing. After whelping, your female dog will be very hungry, so give her as much food as she will eat and as previously said, do not be alarmed if she consumes the expelled placenta.

Vizsla puppies generally weigh between 14 and 20 ounces at birth and when they are born their eyes and ears will be closed. They will also have very little fur, so they are completely dependent on their mother for warmth and care. If you suspect that the pups are not warm enough or are likely to chill over-night, consider getting hold of a heat lamp. This can be sighted above the whelping area. Care must be taken not to overheat either them or the mother. So it is perhaps best to place this at one end or a corner, therefore leaving a part of the whelping area cooler. Be extra health and safety conscious and ensure the heat lamp is not close to anything likely to overheat and combust.

The puppies will spend most of their day nursing and sleeping until their eyes start to open around 3 weeks of age. Between the third and sixth week after birth, is when the puppies will start to become more active, playing with each other and exploring the whelping box area. The puppies will also start to grow very quickly as long as you feed the mother enough so she can produce enough milk.

Around six weeks after birth, is when you should start weaning the puppies, if the mother has not started already. Start to offer the puppies small amounts of puppy food soaked in water or broth to soften it. The puppies may sample a bit of the food, even as they are still nursing, but they should be fully transitioned onto solid food by eight weeks of age. If you do not plan to keep the puppies yourself, it is at this time that you should start introducing the puppies to potential buyers. You should never sell a puppy that has not been fully weaned. You should also carefully vet potential buyers to make sure that the puppies go to a good home.

Puppies are very impressionable during the first few months of life so you need to make sure they get as many experiences (socialization) as possible. If your puppies are not exposed to new things at a young age they will grow up to be fearful and nervous adults. Give the puppies plenty of toys to play with as their teeth start to grow in around week ten and start playing with them yourself so they get used to being handled by humans.

CHAPTER THIRTEEN:

CANINE PSYCHOLOGY - THE VIZSLA MIND

This area of the book is going to talk about true understanding of the Vizsla dog. From carefully reading his body language, to keeping his super intelligent mind busy, you will learn it here.

For too many years, we have either misunderstood our dogs or followed completely inaccurate advice on what our canine friends are thinking. We look to experts that state their knowledge confidently and employ self-proclaimed dog "whisperers" like they have some kind of magic eye.

Thankfully though, we can now obtain a far better understanding of our dogs, simply by exploring all of the research done over the last few years.

As a science in itself, canine understanding has surpassed all previous knowledge and continues to do so. In short we have learned more about the mental and emotional capacity of our dogs in the last ten to twenty years, than we learned in the two hundred previous.

We are lucky enough to be able to study our dogs and know exactly what that eye flick or yawn means, because kind and careful science has worked it out. This huge amount of new knowledge leaves far less need for employment of a dog whisperer or interpreter to tell you how your dog feels.

It makes it possible, with just a small amount of learning from recent research, to understand your dog's basic behavior and needs without the need for any translation.

Knowledge and mutual understanding, between you and your dog, is exactly what this area of the book aims to provide you with.

1.) Vizsla Body Language

This first section is the place where you can learn what your dog's body language is saying. It can be easy to misinterpret some behaviors and acts that our dogs carry out naturally. However, when you have read this part of the book, you will read your dog's behavior in a very different way.

So what is your dog saying with his face, body, posture and tail? Read on to find out;

Eyes

The eyes of this breed will tell you a lot about what he is thinking. To be fair, you will probably know when your dog is anxious and fearful, they simply have a worried stare. A relaxed dog on the other hand, will have a slightly squinty eyes, less startled look, showing that he is happy.

A dog will not usually hold eye contact with you happily, until he has been with you for a long time and feels completely secure to do so.

Some dogs never feel happy to hold eye contact.

Some dogs may stare, and some people believe that this focus is the dog's equivalent of a hug.

A new dog or insecure dog will interpret human eye contact as a worrying event. This can be a learned response or just a natural one but it's quite common. It's usually best not to establish eye contact in this way when you are not absolutely certain that the dog feels secure.

If you stare at a dog that feels insecure, for any amount of time, you will probably see him displaying specific acts that show his unease. He may lick his lips, yawn, look away or raise a paw, this is the dog stating that he is not so keen on your attention being delivered that way.

When is Eye Contact Good

The only exception to eye contact being a worrying affair, is during training sessions, where you are teaching a dog to focus carefully upon you for reward.

This is something you will notice in your training sessions, and is a part of training which naturally builds a dog's confidence.

Half Moon Eyes

If there is any tension or stiffness in his stance and the whites of either of his eyes are showing, then the dog is likely to be uneasy. The white of an eye showing in a 'half-moon" shape is a good early indication that a dog is worried or concerned about something.

Extreme tension, directed focus and an unflinching stare means that the dog is very uneasy. At this point the tension must be broken by taking away any focus from the dog and therefore, diffusing any anxiety that he may feel.

In a lot of cases it is merely part of their learning experience, which is why socialization is so important. The more they are exposed to worrying situations, the more they realize there is nothing to fear, and they no longer react with anxiety.

Body Position and Stance

As a general rule if a dog's body language seems to be leaning back, from the ears to the tail then the dog is relaxed. If everything gives the impression of leaning forwards, from pricked ears (obviously with a Vizsla this isn't so obvious with his floppy ears, but you should still see ear movement, that appears to move forward) to taut body language, then the dog is generally quite aroused.

Hackles, which is the name given to the hair along the dog's back, can bristle if the animal is either worried or anxious. A common misconception is the belief that hackles mean the dog is feeling aggressive but this really is not the case.

The hair will bristle and stand quite high right along the back with aggression. But it can also be a sign that the dog is insecure or unsure in a social situation.

The Tail

The tail of the Vizsla dog tells us a lot about what the animal is thinking. The higher the tail is held the more aroused a dog is.

The tail that is held very low or tucked beneath the dog betrays insecurity; whilst a high tail displays confidence towards an interaction.

If your Vizsla has been docked, the tail will not be as noticeable, but you should still be able to see the general movement up or down.

2.) VIZSLA CALMING SIGNALS

Calming signals are often missed by people even when displayed by their own dogs who have been with them for years. This is because the calming signal is often a very subtle form of communication.

A dog displays calming signals to other dogs and people as a form of specific communication. They also act to calm his own anxiety if he feels worried or insecure.

I recently watched a dog that was tied up outside a store, calming herself with basic signals; although no-one was paying her any attention at all. This particular dog was ***licking her lips*** repeatedly as a way to calm her own anxiety.

Dogs do this along with ***yawning*** and ***flicking their eyes*** to one side very briefly if they feel anxious. These three actions are the main calming signals that dogs display on a regular basis.

A well socialized dog will recognize the briefest calming signal from another. In this case they usually respond with kindness by acting in a way that diffuses the anxiety of the worried dog.

A dog that has not learned to read the language of other canines, perhaps because of a lack of early socialization, will probably ignore polite calming signals and dive in to greet the insecure dog. This can increase the anxiety of the situation and in some cases, lead to dog fights.

Alongside the three already mentioned, other common calming signals include;

* A very slight paw lift
* Turning away
* Whining
* Dipping the head

* Seeming to focus on something away in the distance

* Sneezing

* Shaking the body as if shaking off water

All of the above are generally mild signals that a Vizsla dog will display during interaction, particularly if the dog is feeling a bit worried, yet not quite stressed.

Strong Calming Signals

The dog that displays strong calming signals may yawn or pant heavily; try to escape the situation or even take a confrontational stance in order to defend himself.

This type of behavior will come after mild calming signals, and before the dog is severely stressed.

The dog will need to be removed from the situation, or the trigger of the behavior will need to be taken away, before the dog is able to calm down. It is important not to just expect the dog to get used to the scary trigger, or this can result in fearful aggression.

How many adults or children have you seen trying to make friends with a scared dog by looming over the poor animal and trying to be reassuring? Even when the poor, increasingly anxious dog is backing off or growling? When really the dog would be far happier if he was just ignored and allowed to get used to the strange human in his own time. This type of scenario is what most often leads to a bitten child or even adult.

3.) Appeasement Behavior

Another type of behavior that a dog may display, particularly the younger of the breed, is appeasement behavior. This type of action involves the dog trying to diffuse any tension in an interaction, in a very puppy like way.

Appeasement behavior is a very natural act which is usually the dog communicating that he wants to be friends; wants no trouble, or is sorry that he was out of line.

Common appeasement behavior types are:

* Jumping up

* Urination on greeting

* Rolling over

* Tucking the tail under

* Muzzle licking, as a puppy does to its mother

Early and continuous socialization is usually the best way to avoid this; or at least make the more mature under-socialized dog more confident.

How Dogs Greet Each Other

Well-mannered greeting between dogs is actually quite different to the way that people greet each other. Dogs that respectfully greet each other, can almost seem to be ignoring the presence of the other animal.

The body will curve around, which is a sign of good manners. A respectful dog will never approach another head on, as this is a sign of disrespect. Sadly it is also how socially awkward dogs approach everyone and everything. It is also the way that people approach each other, and the way that they approach dogs.

4.) Dealing with Social Fear

We can take action to modify fear behavior, and eventually change it into relaxed behavior.

In some cases dog trainers have wrongly advised that to get a dog feeling happy, in a scary situation, they must flood the dog's senses with a stimulus until the dog eventually learns to cope.

About Flooding

Flooding was once considered a viable method of helping a dog to recover from fear.

The idea was that the exposure to the stimulus becomes so intense that the dog will eventually pass the point of fear into relaxation, and the fear will be 'fixed'.

It has since been learned that this is not the case. The behavior which was formerly identified as improvement, was actually complete mental shutdown; which is worse for the dog than the fear itself.

About Masking

Masking is the act of putting the dog into the situation, yet threatening him or hurting him if he reacts to it. This is often seen in dominance based dog training. The dog is forced to wear an inhumane collar, or threatened with violence, and pushed into a scary or stress filled situation.

An improvement may be seen at the time, because the collar/handler threatens the already stressed dog into mental shutdown. But the behavior has not been truly modified, just temporarily disabled. The dog still feels the same, and often even worse, about the trigger when treated this way.

How the Experts Modify Social Fear

The act of modifying social fear, is to gently change the dog's impression of the frightening encounter, stimulus or scary environment. This is a case of rewarding relaxed behavior when the dog is in the presence of something which worries him.

Whether the act of reward is carried out when the dog is ten paces from it, or fifty paces away from the stimulus, depends on how close a dog can be to the source of his fear whilst staying relaxed. Similarly, progress will be dictated by the dog's ability to stay relaxed, as he gets closer to the stimulus.

In everyday life, this is a case of building the dog's confidence gently, and at a pace which he can handle.

With this approach we can gradually get closer to the worrying stimulus by rewarding relaxation as you go. If the dog's behavior begins to change, then he has been taken too close too soon.

We can use treats, special toys, praise and attention to help a dog stay relaxed.

The Overall Approach

The first thing we do is really observe the dog. See exactly what sets his behavior off; because only by knowing this can we start to improve things. The thing that sets the behavior off is called a trigger.

The first behavior that a dog will show when he becomes aware of something worrying is calming signals. In extreme cases, the dog may react with fear or terror and want to run away.

Remember that common calming signals include;

* Licking lips
* Yawning
* Glancing away

This is the point of necessary action, because calming signals mean that the dog is uncomfortable in some way. In this case, they mean that he is becoming anxious, because of the presence of the trigger.

So, it is important to move as far away as the dog needs to be from the thing that worries him; in order for relaxation to re-occur and be rewarded. Again, once the dog shows signs of relaxation and self control, you must praise and reward the behavior. Gradually get them closer to the fearful trigger, and attempt to stay there longer each time.

It can take a long time; but is the only way to change a dog's emotional response and social fear permanently, and in a positive way.

5.) VIZSLA TRAINING – HOW DOES HE LEARN

Your dog's behavior is part genetic influence, yet mostly environmental conditioning. Again, from the moment he is conceived, the dog's behavior is being shaped This is the first step of environmental conditioning, and this learning never stops. Although it has a huge surge in the period between birth and adulthood.

How exactly does a dog learn?

Canine training and therefore his learning, is a process of receiving rewards. If a dog finds that something he does is rewarded, then he will repeat it. If the dog finds that the same behavior provides no reward at all then the behavior will not be repeated. Any dog merely wishes to please their guardian, so logically they will refrain from behavior that displeases you.

Where this becomes complicated, is the examination of reward.

The most obvious type of reward are the classic ones; food, treats, toys, games and verbal praise. All of these, timed carefully will teach a dog to repeat a behavior, but so will other things too. These are the responses that happen by accident, but teach the dog anyway.

Inadvertent rewards are slightly different. They are things that you may not think classically reward your dog.

The following are examples of inadvertent rewards that can easily teach any dog bad habits;

* The mailman retreating when the dog barks (relieving anxiety about an intruder)

* Pushing a dog off when he jumps up (interaction)

* Shouting at a dog as he barks (interaction)

* Passing the dog a morsel from your plate when he asks (food)

Inadvertent rewarding experiences, such as the ones above, are the biggest part of canine learning. Unless we know what to look for we have no idea that our dogs are being rewarded by their environment. This leaves us confused as to why our dogs are developing problematic habits.

When your dog learns something from a response within his or her environment, the response is called a 'reinforcer' because it makes a behavior stronger.

Reinforcement may seem quite confusing at first, yet it is well worth taking some time to understand. When you can understand the details of reinforcement, then you will have a flawless knowledge on exactly how your dog learns from his or her environment.

Environmental Learning in Dogs

As a whole story, the dog learns from his environment in four separate ways. Everything that happens to the dog that he learns from, will be one of these four ways. Whether planned or unplanned, set-up or accidental, your Vizsla will learn from them just the same.

By understanding the following, you will understand exactly how your dog learns new things.

1) Positive Reinforcement

Something good starts.

Positive reinforcement describes an act that adds something. When the dog is behaving in a certain way and is rewarded, this will strengthen the behavior. For instance if you give the dog food as he sits, then he is more likely to sit again.

The dog that is fed treats in a training session to reinforce a specific behavior is being trained with positive reinforcement.

2) Negative Reinforcement

Something bad stops.

Negative reinforcement is the act of something being taken away, or stopping, when the dog changes his behavior.

For instance the dog that is pulling on the leash whilst wearing a pinch collar learns that when he stops pulling, the pinching stops too.

3) Positive Punishment

Something bad starts.

Positive punishment describes something being added to a behavior in order to teach the dog not to carry out the behavior again.

For instance, if a dog barks and I quickly squirt him with water so that he stops, I have used positive punishment.

4) Negative Punishment

Something good stops.

Negative punishment describes the act of taking something away when a behavior is carried out. This is used to show the dog that if he behaves a certain way, something that he likes will be lost.

So if a dog is being played with and nips your hand. You then take away the act of playing with him; the dog should quickly learn not to nip or the game will end. It is important to note here why it is necessary to phase out food rewards gradually. If you suddenly stop giving treats when he has been used to it for so long, then he is likely to feel confused and that he is perhaps being punished.

Which Is The Best Method For Training A Vizsla?

Each of these learning methods will work if carried out to perfection. Yet some methods are kinder than others. In this book we will not be using positive punishment (***something bad starts***) nor will we use negative reinforcement (***something bad stops)***.

We avoid these training methods, purely because we want our dogs to be happy. Happy dogs should not be subject to ***'bad things'*** happening in their training sessions.

Positive reinforcement (***something good starts)***, and negative punishment (***something good stops)***, can be combined perfectly to teach your Vizsla dog everything that he needs to know about the world.

These methods can be used to carefully modify unhelpful behaviors, and to teach useful behavior in every aspect of your life with your dog.

A Note on Positive Punishment

There is another reason why we will not be using positive punishment in this book. The method can have an opposite effect on a behavior to the one which is planned.

By its very nature, positive punishment requires the dog to carry out a particular behavior in order for it to be punished. Each time a behavior is carried out it is practiced, and every time a behavior is practiced it is strengthened.

Therefore by punishing a dog each time he does something, we are allowing him to do it; therefore to learn it, and this increases the likelihood of a repeated act.

For instance if the dog barks at passers-by and we add a squirt of water to his face every time he barks, we are actually doing nothing to change the behavior itself. We are simply allowing the same train of thought which the dog always has, leading up to a frenzied torrent of barking, to remain the same.

Thus we are actually expecting the dog to either change his own behavior or foresee ours before deciding how to respond to a passer-by. It's a big expectation for any dog, who are by nature well-known to live in the moment.

Which is exactly why positive punishment is a poor method when trying to train a Vizsla or any dog at all.

6.) HOW ATTENTION WORKS

One of the most common ways that we add positive reinforcement to a behavior is with attention. Dogs adore attention from the people they love. The reason that attention will shape a dog's behavior, is because it is positive reinforcement in action.

Negative attention works in exactly the same way as positive attention. Which means that whether you tell a dog that he is good, or shout at him for being bad; when he carries out an act, you are still giving him attention that he craves. Positive reinforcement merely makes the act stronger.

Any dog with a behavior problem such as jumping up or barking, that is constantly corrected with attention, is being rewarded for the behavior. In other words, the fact that you respond to the dog, albeit in a negative way, the dog is still getting the attention it craves.

Because attention is so easy to give to our dogs, attention seeking behavior can become a real problem.

When the dog looks at you and barks. When he steals things and chews them up whilst you are trying to take them off him. And when he jumps up constantly, he is displaying attention seeking behavior.

I once had a situation with two West Highland White Terriers that would guard whoever was on the sofa. So whichever dog it was, would growl at the other dog, warning it off. If I touched the dog sat next to me, the growling and snarling got worse. This wasn't aggression that was in anyway directed at me, but purely directed at the other dog. However, as soon as I learned to ignore this, and particularly as soon as I stood up, the dog had lost its focus and reinforcement. They would literally look around at each other, wondering what they were going to do next.

This type of behavior works if it brings attention, therefore a cycle is established. ***Take a look;***

* When we tell a dog that is barking, to be quiet, we are actually rewarding the dog for the bark. (telling it to be quiet is giving it attention)

* Pushing a dog away when he jumps up is a rewarding process. We are giving him physical and emotional attention.

* We chase the dog around the park calling his name. He has our full attention and a great game too.

* We may have been previously ignoring the dog, and so he picks up something he shouldn't have, and we give him attention.

Dogs generally do what we teach them to do by our responses. How does the dog feel though? Take a look at my example here;

A particular dog is becoming a nuisance when jumping up. He recently knocked someone over and his whole family are covered in bruises. The dog has always jumped up; he learned it as a puppy. Back then it was encouraged, because he was much smaller, and the act was far less intrusive. He knows his guardian is not happy with him jumping up because they seem to be angry when he does it.

Yet it used to make them happy, so the dog tries harder and harder to bring back that happy reaction. Also, his guardian is touching him and speaking to him (albeit in a frustrated way); and the dog likes that, because he loves this person. Now unless something in the owner's response changes, the dog will continue to provoke that exact response by jumping up.

This type of innate learning causes most of what the dog has learned so far in his life. As dog caretakers we must take responsibility for the way the dogs in our homes act. For our dogs take their guidance from us, and us alone.

To raise a nicely mannered puppy, it's a really good idea to monitor your own delivery of attention. Remember that attention causes repeat behavior; and lack of attention will give the dog no reason to repeat his act.

If you follow this rule and make a habit of it, then you will be carefully shaping many of your dog's behaviors with little effort at all.

Extinction – Stop That Behavior for Good!

So what can we do about behavior that has already been learned? And how can we apply the rule of reinforcement to that?

Well, if attention causes a behavior to be repeated, and lack of attention gives the dog no reason to repeat his behavior (my previous Westie example), a simple shift of attention will make a great deal of difference.

First of all though let's take a look at extinction.

Extinction is the name given to anything that goes away and does not come back. In behavior terms, this means the act that ceases to be repeated, such as jumping up or begging at the table.

If a behavior goes un-rewarded for long enough, the dog will display something called an extinction burst where the act gets momentarily worse. Shortly after that, the act will go away altogether, a result known as extinction.

At this point it is therefore vital for the dog owner not to give in, for success is closer than it has ever been!

The reason that extinction is often not reached, is because the dog owner often gives in and responds to the extinction burst, thinking that ignoring the behavior is not working. When the increase in behavior is actually showing that not only is it working, but that the approach is almost complete.

When working towards extinction, the other thing to introduce is more attention to the behavior you want. This will take focus from the unwanted behavior and make him keener to produce good behavior.

Chapter Fourteen:

Vizsla Behavior Problems.

In this area of the book I wanted to talk about potential, breed specific, behavior problems that the Vizsla may develop. Like people, dogs have their own specific personalities. The behavior that the Vizsla displays is partly based on his nature, and mostly a result of the nurturing effect that life has had on him so far. Most canine problems can be halted before they get too severe, or even modified into manageable acts. It's important to have an understanding of behavior before trying to make any changes.

1.) Dealing with Common Behavior Problems

The Vizsla is a fairly high-maintenance breed that requires a great deal of exercise and interaction with family. If your dog doesn't get enough exercise or attention he is likely to develop problem behaviors which may require professional training to correct. What you need to understand before you try to tackle any behavior problem, is that many behaviors that you might consider problematic are actually natural behaviors for your dog.

For example, chewing is a very natural way for puppies to learn about their world. They also do it to ease the pain of teething. When your puppy fulfills his need to chew by gnawing on an expensive pair of shoes, is when the behavior becomes a problem. The best way to deal with problem behaviors is not to teach your puppy to avoid the behavior altogether but to channel that behavior toward a more appropriate outlet. Below you will find tips for dealing with some of the most common behavior problems in dogs:

Chewing – The best way to keep your Vizsla from chewing on things he shouldn't be chewing on is to make sure that he has plenty of toys available. Many dogs chew on things out of boredom, so ensuring that your Vizsla gets enough exercise and play time, will also help to keep him from chewing on things around the house. If chewing does become a problem all you need to do is replace the item your dog is chewing on with one of his toys (swapping). Ideally you would have taken care of such items in your initial puppy proofing stage. However, we can't always be sure which he will chew and which he will ignore. You are therefore better off keeping every potential chewable item that you wish to keep intact, out of his reach.

If after this you still find your Vizsla has found something you had forgotten about and is chewing on it, tell him "No" in a firm tone and take the object away. Immediately replace the object with your dog's favorite toy, then praise him when he starts chewing on it. Eventually your Vizsla will learn what he is and is not allowed to chew on around the house.

Digging – Just like chewing, digging is a behavior that dogs often exhibit when they are bored. While digging is a natural behavior for dogs, it becomes problematic when your Vizsla chooses to do it in the middle of your favorite flower bed, or under your fence. A simple way to deal with this problem is to provide your Vizsla with a small section of the yard where he is allowed to dig. Bury a few toys or treats in the area to encourage your Vizsla to dig there. If you find your Vizsla digging in the yard, tell him "No" in a firm voice and lead him away from the area and into his special digging zone. Reward and praise him when he starts to dig there instead. If this becomes particularly problematic, you may simply have to fence off any such areas.

Jumping Up – We have already covered this to an extent elsewhere, but go into a bit more depth here. What many dog owners do not realize is that they actually teach their dogs to jump up on people when they come in the door or when the dog gets excited. When your

Vizsla is a cute and cuddly puppy it can be tempting to reward him with pets and cuddles when he crawls into your lap or jumps up at your legs. When your Vizsla grows up, he expects you to react in the same way to this behavior because you have reinforced it. In order to curb this problem behavior you simply need to teach your Vizsla that jumping up will not get him what he wants; your attention.

The Vizsla is a very affectionate breed with family, but he can be a little wary around strangers unless properly socialized. For this reason, jumping up is not a behavioral problem that is particularly common with the Vizsla but it is still possible. To teach your Vizsla not to jump up on people, you may need to enlist the help of a friend or two. Have your friends stand outside the front door to your house and ring the doorbell. This should get your Vizsla excited. After ringing the doorbell, have your friend enter the house. When your Vizsla jumps up, your friend should place their hands behind their back and ignore the dog for a few seconds before turning around and leaving again.

After a few repetitions of this, have your friend give your Vizsla the "Sit" command. If he complies, allow your friend to calmly pet the dog for a few seconds before leaving again. Repeat this sequence several times until your Vizsla remains calm when the doorbell rings. It may take quite a few repetitions to recondition your dog against jumping up, but with consistency you can make it happen.

Whining – Similar to jumping up on you, your Vizsla's whining has one goal; to get your attention. When your Vizsla whines at you, stand up calmly and leave the room; go into another room and close the door. Wait for a few seconds until your Vizsla stops whining, then return to the room and pet him calmly. Repeat this sequence every time your dog whines at you, and he will eventually learn that whining does not earn him your attention.

Barking – In most cases Vizslas are not an overly loud breed, but some dogs tend to bark more than others; especially when they get excited. The easiest way to teach your dog to stop barking is actually to teach him to bark on command first. Again, you will need to have a friend stand outside your front door and to ring the doorbell. Get your Vizsla's attention and give him the "Speak" command. As soon as you give the command, have your friend ring the doorbell to get your dog to bark. When he does, praise him

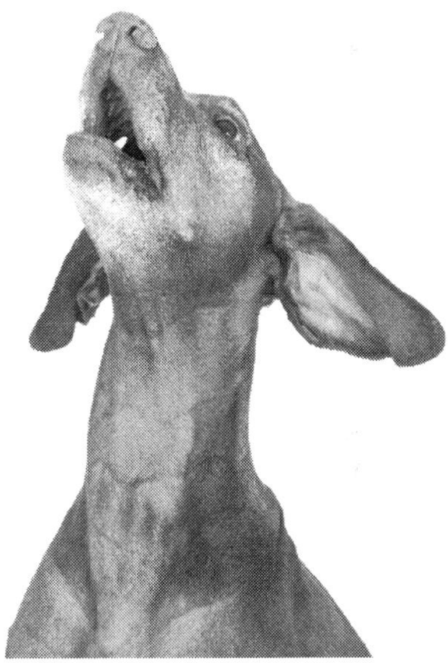

excitedly and reward him. After a few repetitions, your dog should start barking on command before the doorbell rings.

Once your dog learns to bark on command you can then teach him a "Hush" command. Give your Vizsla the "Speak" command and let him bark a few times before telling him "Hush". When he stops barking, praise him and offer him a treat. Repeat this sequence several times until your Vizsla gets the hang of it. Vizslas are an intelligent breed that will be eager to please, so this shouldn't take too many repetitions.

So to recap, first teach the dog to bark and add a command ("Speak/ Bark") to it. Next, start to reinforce the short pauses between barks and add a command ("Hush/Quiet") to THEM. The dog will learn that the pauses are rewarded too; therefore he is rewarded for being quiet as well as to bark. But he must learn to bark on command first of all, before being taught to be quiet on command. As with any of your previous training, it is important to mark the behavior so that there is no confusion and your dog knows exactly what is expected.

Again the command word can be 'quiet' or 'be quiet'. Remember to be quick with this next bit of making him quiet. You want him to know at what point he receives a treat for being quiet. What you will hopefully get to, is the stage where you are no longer rewarding the barking, but you ARE rewarding the 'quiet'. In this way he shouldn't be so keen to bark, particularly if he knows there is no treat to follow. Of course, it is unlikely that you will stop the natural impulse for him to bark, but at least now, you should be able to quickly stop him.

The second option is better for a dog who doesn't bark very much. Once again the clicker is a great tool, but what you need to do this time, is show the dog his reward and encourage him to offer behaviors that will earn him the reward.

He will go through his repertoire in order to try and get the treat from you. Eventually he will make a sound, it may not be a bark it may not even be a growl, just a squeak. The most important thing to do is reward any sound. That sound can then be shaped into a bark by then gently withholding a reward bit by bit until the dog barks. It is kind of teasing the dog, but is only necessary in these initial stages. A lot of people use this when you want to give them a treat for no apparent reason, but you wish the dog to "ask" for it. So they say something like, 'say please', whilst they are offering the treat. Obviously you only give the treat when they bark.

It may seem odd to teach your dog to bark when you wish them to stop. The point of this is that YOU are in control, telling him to either bark or stop barking. What you are doing is 'tricking' the dog into stopping with his barking, by your command/reward approach. Of course once he has mastered the 'stop barking' command, you are unlikely to need the 'start barking' command. So again, I am not suggesting that you will ever stop a dog from barking, particularly a dog with a high predisposition to bark. What you will have with this training approach however, is more control and the ability to stop him sooner.

2.) Will He Chase The Cat?

The answer to this question really has many variables. An adult Vizsla that has never encountered cats may well give chase. A puppy that is brought home and introduced to a bold and confident cat immediately, will probably not. The elderly dog that lived with a cat in his previous home may not chase either.

Cats can generally stand their ground with all but the most determined and tenacious dogs. They use the needles on their feet very well. Most dogs that chase cats, do so often because the cat is already running away. As you already know, dogs loves games involving a chase.

If you live with a cat, (or really any small animal, rabbit, hamster etc), and are bringing home a new dog it is important to carry out careful introductions. The best idea is to give the cat somewhere high to sit and observe the dog below. It is not a good idea to introduce a dog and cat without giving the cat an escape route. In the case of the other small animal, it is best to keep them safely in their cage/enclosure at first.

It may take some time for your cat to get used to the new dog. Or they may get on really well straightaway. Cross species relationships are usually quite successful if the two animals are introduced carefully, and have been well socialized.

3.) Teething

If you live with a Vizsla puppy you must be prepared for teething time.

As his adult teeth begin to come through at a few months old your puppy will be desperate to chew things.

The baby teeth will probably either be swallowed or lost as the new teeth come through from underneath. It's unusual to find a puppy tooth but you might.

It is a great idea to provide the teething puppy with his own toys for this difficult time. Pet stores have a vast array of puppy teething toys, and it's worth buying your dog at least two or three of different materials.

In addition you can give your puppy a plastic bottle with frozen water in or some suitably sized ice cubes made with stock and frozen. This will soothe the hot gums, whilst the teeth are coming through.

Carrots too are great teething chews, along with being a healthy snack that might just save your best shoes.

It's important to note here that even with teething toys, your puppy may still find electrical cables an attractive alternative. As mentioned in the puppy proofing section, never allow your puppy access to any electrical cabling. If you cannot sufficiently hide these, then unplug and preferably tie these up out of harms reach. You do not need me to point out the obvious that a chewed live cable, could result in a fatality.

4.) Bite Inhibition

Bite inhibition is one of the reasons that a dog must stay with his or her mother for at least the first seven to eight weeks of life. What is bite inhibition though and how does it affect your life with the Vizsla dog?

In the litter, and when interacting with his mother, the puppy first learns to inhibit his own bite. When suckling from his mother she will correct the young puppy if his teeth are used too freely.

Similarly later on, at three weeks old and beyond, the puppy can expect to be corrected by his siblings if he nips too hard during friendly interaction and play.

From the aforementioned interactions, the puppy learns that he can touch his immediate canine family with his teeth but must not nip too hard, for this will get him into trouble.

When you bring the puppy home it is important to continue this learning. For the first few days you can allow your puppy to put his teeth onto your hands in a controlled manner. If the puppy bites too hard though it is important to correct the behavior with a sharp sound "NO" and stern stare, as his mother and siblings would do. Again, never attempt to hit or even tap his nose, as this can have an adverse affect.

After that first few days you can begin to teach the puppy that his own toys and chews are a far more suitable plaything than human skin. Redirect any nipping behavior onto a toy and your puppy will get the idea quite quickly.

The reason that bite inhibition learning must be a two stage process is that the dog is eventually taught not to bite people. Before though, he must learn that for some reason, if he ever feels that he has to bite in order to survive then he must do the least damage possible.

5)A Note on Growling

It is important to know your own dog, where growling is concerned.

Take a look at the scenario within which the growl occurs. Observe your dog's body language and the signs that show how he must be feeling, before deciding why your dog may be growling.

Generally in the dog world, growling is an early warning system that something is not right. The growl from an aggressive dog can be delivered seconds before a bite.

If a dog growls at your approach or attention, then it is a request to be left alone. You should adhere to that, for the dog has very few methods of communicating his wishes.

Dog growling during play and tug games is actually common. So if your Vizsla growls when he is playing, it is probably him expressing himself rather than a display of aggression. Although it can sound pretty fierce, play based growling is usually nothing to worry about.

6) Resource Guarding

Resource guarding is something that any dog can develop, but it is usually as a result of a learning experience. A dog that has been truly hungry for instance is likely to develop resource guarding of food which may settle when the dog feels secure, or it may not.

a)Fear Guarding

When a dog is scared of losing a resource he may be reactive to anyone who approaches the resource. He may growl or even bite. To then approach the dog and focus on the resource, is doing nothing more than intensifying the fear. Therefore, the dog is likely to be more aggressive, not less.

When resource guarding is based on fear, confrontation is the last thing that will end the behavior. Fear aggression is actually the one within which a dog is most likely to bite.

Take a second to imagine how you would feel if you were really worried about losing something. Then I came along and threatened you in order to take it away. Now imagine if you think your survival depended on that resource. Would you fight me for it? I suspect that you would.

This is exactly how a dog feels when he is resource guarding through fear.

Now imagine for a moment how you would feel if I approached and offered more of the resource that you were scared of losing. Imagine if I offered an abundance and simultaneously paid no attention to your resource at all. How would you feel then? I suspect that if I flooded your general area with many similar resources, and took none away, you would begin to relax.

This is exactly the approach that we take with a dog that is scared of losing his food, and so guards it. We put a few different food bowls down which are a good distance apart, then we add food into each of them in order to make up the dog's entire meal.

It is important to begin by keeping a distance until eventually the dog is aware that each time a bowl is approached, something nice is going into it.

B) Swapping

If you are raising a Vizsla puppy, then it is a good idea to teach swapping very early on. Every dog should know how to swap, because this is a good and fair way to take something away from the dog, that he shouldn't have.

When you play with toys then swap regularly, retrieving with balls is a really good way to practice this. You can show the dog that you are happy to throw the next ball just as soon as he has handed over the one he just fetched back.

C) Stealing

The dog that steals things and refuses to give them back will benefit from learning to swap too. The important thing to remember with this, is that the behavior is likely to stem from attention seeking, maybe even boredom.

Therefore if your dog is stealing things to get your attention, you may be better off ignoring the behavior as it will eventually become extinct. If you go for this approach, remember to keep all valuables out of the dogs reach, otherwise you may have no choice but give in to an extinction burst.

Attention seeking behavior that results in stealing, is the only behavior where the dog shouldn't be given something else.

The attention seeker is best completely ignored when he is guarding a resource, because this can cause the behavior to be repeated.

D) I Am His Resource – This Dog Guards Me

This can happen around other people and/or dogs. It is therefore important, in everyday life, that the dog is well socialized and taught relaxed behavior around other people and dogs.

Any overly aggressive behavior in this circumstance really needs to be carefully monitored.

It is usually associated with under socialization and resource guarding. It is unlikely, but if serious aggression occurs, then this is best viewed by a local and qualified professional dog behaviorist.

7) The Dog Hates the Car

This can happen with any dog breed, so again is not necessarily breed specific.

Hyperactive behavior in the car can be as a result of general fear, or specific sight enhancement.

The cars going by so quickly or a general flooding of the senses can over stimulate a dog, leaving them quite anxious. Even the puppy that has been socialized in the car can possibly develop this distracted behavior later on.

There are some things to try when travelling with your dog which may help;

* Herbal sickness remedies; if your dog is being or feeling sick, then remedies may help in the short term to make him feel better when travelling.

* Rescue remedy; this Bach flower remedy may just take the edge off the anxiety when travelling; enough that your dog can relax.

* A crate and blanket; putting your dog in a crate and covering it with a blanket may prevent the behavior developing. With this approach, the dog never gets to see the movement from the car window.

You can also try teaching the dog to stop barking on command as previously discussed but the stimulation beyond the car windows may simply be too much for the dog to cope with, and this approach may not work.

8) My Dog Won't Come Back

As previously mentioned in the chapter on training even the very best behaved pet will suffer if he isn't given the opportunity for a daily walk/run. A bored dog will become depressed, destructive or even aggressive. It is thought that some dog owners refrain from giving their dogs the off lead runs they need for fear that the dog won't come back when called. It is great that an owner cares for the dogs safety, but is not really helping the dog receive vital exercise.

Please again refer back to Chapter Six, Training your Vizsla dog and specifically the section of obedience training, "Come". Following the instructions and guidance there, should solve this problem.

9) Fears and Phobias

Whether they have lived in a safe home since puppy-hood, or were raised in a different environment, any dog can develop fear behaviors. Fireworks, thunder, travel, other animals and people are some examples of why your dog can become afraid.

A dog that is fearful has a very distinct body language. He will tuck his tail below his hind quarters and cower. He may try to leave the situation and look away from the frightening stimulus. It is vital that a scared dog is never cornered.

A scared or worried dog will often display calming signals. We have covered these in a previous chapter, and again, these are signals that dogs use in order to diffuse a worrying situation. Some calming signals as previously mentioned include yawning; a stressed dog will yawn frequently.

The yawning response is often mistaken for tiredness by an uninformed human. However, once you know what to look for, it is easily recognizable. Licking his lips; a calming signal and stress response, can take the form of a single nose lick or more. Sniffing the ground is a "leave me alone, I am invisible" plea.

Your job as the owner of a fearful dog is to neither ignore nor encourage the fear. Be aware of the situations in which your dog feels threatened and gently build him up, so that he can cope better with them. Introduce new and worrying situations gradually, and amalgamate them with rewards such as playing with a toy or receiving a treat for relaxed behavior.

A very important point is to never over sympathize with your dog as this can reinforce the fear. If he gets too much attention when he is afraid, he will either repeat the behavior for the attention, or even worse think that the stimulus is a threat which you too recognize. If he sees that the stimulus doesn't concern you, then your dog will learn that it shouldn't concern him either.

A scared dog should never be cornered or forced to accept attention. If he is, then he will become more scared, growl and possibly even snap. It is better to help him relax around people without them paying him any attention, than to push him into a negative reaction.

If the fear has an environmental cause, for instance fireworks then it is worth trying a natural remedy to appease your dog's fear. Rescue remedy which can be bought in most chemists/drug stores, is suitable for short-term treatment of a worried dog. Your vet may also be able to suggest something to get your dog through difficult times such as on bonfire night or New Year's Eve, when there are a lot of fireworks.

10) Dogs and Children

Most dogs that have been brought up with children, manage really well in a family environment. It's worth remembering that if an adult dog has never encountered children, he may find them worrying. They do, after all, move differently to adults and sound different.

If you have a dog that is worried about children, it is really important that you make your pet feel safe and secure when there are children around. And for both the dog and child's sake never take any risks. You can get children to give the dog treats, otherwise completely ignore him. He ideally needs to get used to them in his own time.

Never under any circumstance, leave a dog with a young child. There are too many cases of dogs attacking children. Dogs can be unpredictable, and children do not have the awareness that an adult has in being able to read signals that the dog needs to be left alone. Sometimes children see dogs as a toy to play with. Dogs can soon tire of a child's constant attention. It is best to teach the child that they have to respect the dog and not unnecessarily tease or harass the dog.

11) Rolling in Poop

What can you do to stop your Vizsla rolling in feces and coming home stinking of poop?

The only real option you have in this circumstance is to increase your control and watch your dog carefully.

The act of rolling in poop is an innate behavior which means it is part of their genetic nature. The good news is that although the behavior is natural, even the worst habits can be changed.

Your job is to ensure you have the most possible control over your dog on walks and can recall him back easily. Then it's simply a case of watching him carefully whenever he is near an area where he may roll. You then simply call him back when he shows any interest in the smelly stuff.

The more recall practice and training that you carry out, the easier it will be to call your dog back when he spots something smelly.

Obviously if the worse happens, then your only option is to give him a bath and thoroughly dry him.

I have only ever had one dog roll in anything, and it was in fact the carcass of a dead fox. The Lurcher in question, took great delight in rolling in the remains. I don't know whether it was an instinctive celebration of the death of an enemy, or something else. Most of the time, of all the dogs I have ever walked, they all seem to seek out other dogs feces and simply scent mark the pile by urinating on it.

12) Separation Anxiety

Separation anxiety is when a dog fears being alone to the point of becoming severely stressed or distressed.

It is currently thought to be for one of an unknown number of reasons. There are two types of separation anxiety, amid other undefined reasons for the disorder. These are fear of unexpected noises or over attachment to the owner.

There is no evidence of this if dogs are left with other dogs and therefore finding any relief from additional canine company. This type of anxiety seems to be linked specifically with the absence of human presence from the home. As every dog is an individual, so is their experience when suffering from separation anxiety.

Some suffer greatly and become destructive to themselves and their surroundings. Others simply become sad and depressed when left alone. They leave no trace of the stress, thus leaving owners unaware that anxiety occurred at all during the dog's alone time.

The actual anxiety becomes a phobia and can become so severe that the dog develops serious stress related behaviors causing poor health, self-harm and obsessive worrying about being left alone. Dogs associate this with the behavior of their owners, and become stressed very early, in regular routines that lead to alone time.

To prevent separation anxiety in your own dog you have a number of options. The best one, if you are leaving your dog regularly, is to employ a willing neighbor or relative to periodically check in on your dog. Alternatively a doggy day caretaker or similar canine professional. This usually takes the form of a canine crèche area or similar and is wonderful for meeting the dog's mental and physical needs alongside ensuring the dog is not alone regularly for long periods of time.

A dog walker is the minimum provision that a full time, at home dog, should have when everyone is out at work all day.

The other possibility here is having two dogs. Companionship can make all the difference, whereby the dogs keep each other company and entertained. However, this doesn't always work and some dogs can still become overwhelmed with separation anxiety, resulting in the aforementioned negative behaviors.

If separation anxiety becomes a real problem, a local dog behaviorist may be the answer. They can observe your dog and create a modification program to try and alleviate his stressed reaction to being alone. This can work really well when carried out carefully.

13) CHASING BEHAVIOR

Chasing wildlife, livestock or similar animals, can be a problem with most dog breeds. Just as other animals are easy targets, so are cars, pedestrians and bikes.

Chasing behavior can also be a really dangerous game with potential fatal consequences. In the UK for example, a farmer is legally entitled to shoot a dog chasing wildlife.

If the behavior is displayed at a dangerous level, you may need to find help locally from a dog trainer/behaviorist. Otherwise you can teach your dog that looking towards you, when he sees something he would normally chase after, is his most rewarding option. Of course this is dependent on you being vigilant and second guessing a potential chase.

You may initially need to provide extra motivation (favorite treat etc) to break your dog's attention away from whatever he is planning to chase.

The steps that we take to reform chasing behavior are similar to those which we use for social fear.

It is a gradual process of teaching the dog to stay relaxed with the trigger at a distance. You also need to Teach the dog to focus on you because you are extremely interesting. Eventually you build the dog's capacity to be near the trigger whilst he also stays relaxed and controlled.

It's important to focus on your dog's behavior carefully, and reinforce every time he looks towards you instead of at the trigger. If you can master this art alone, then your control over the behavior of your Vizsla dog will improve dramatically.

It is important too that you don't allow him to do any chasing at all if you can help it. If you have to put him on the leash in risky areas then do that rather than allow your dog to enjoy the chase. Again, anticipation is the key here.

Any dog that gets the chance to chase squirrels, rabbits or other animals, is strengthening the desire to chase them and repeated practices of chase behavior can easily become obsession.

14) AGGRESSION

The Vizsla as a dog breed, although relatively friendly, can potentially deal with worrying situations with an aggressive response. Aggressive behavior is worrying to us as owners. There are many types of aggression but most of them are caused by fear for one reason or another.

A dog's body language will usually change greatly before he becomes aggressive.

The process from fear to bite will go something like this;

* The dog will focus on the stimulant (the thing that he's worried about) Calming signals will follow, the dog may glance away, yawn or try to leave the situation. If the calming signals do not take away the stimulant, the dog will then change his posture, shift his bodyweight, his hackles may raise and he may growl.

* If growling doesn't work the dog will show his teeth. If flashing the teeth doesn't work he may snap at the air between him and the stimulant.

* The next thing that may occur is that the dog may freeze. This is a very brief act and can be missed if you're not looking for it. The freeze is the dog making a decision to either fight or flee the threat. If he can't leave the situation or the stimulant is not removed, the dog is at severe risk of biting. This is because he feels he has no choice, and to be fair, he has given a lot of warning.

Some dogs, as an exception to the above, have learned to cope so well with their fears that they don't even show that they're scared or uncomfortable before the aggression manifests.

This is because the reaction of aggression has been used by the dog for so long that he relies on it as a default reaction to fear. This dog will bypass everything and go straight to aggression. Any dog that does this, needs to be seen by a qualified behaviorist.

A) AGGRESSION TO DOGS

Dog to dog aggression can be based in lack of socialization. In other words they are unsure of and therefore potentially fearful of other dogs. The dog simply does not know how to behave around other canines so he becomes scared, and in turn uses attack as a form of defence. Often a dog will seem to be aggressive towards others when really he is not thinking of fighting at all; he just doesn't know what else to do.

b) Aggression to People

Aggression towards people is often fear of the person that the aggression is aimed towards. It could also be general fear of the situation which the dog is dealing with at the time. An example is a dog in kennels that shows his teeth through the bars because he's scared and confused.

I have only touched on the basics of aggression here, there is so much information that the subject could fill an entire book.

The main thing to remember though is to observe your dog and if you feel he may be uncomfortable or unhappy in this situation watch out for the process described above and proceed as described.

15) A Local Dog Trainer

If you are having serious problems with the behavior of your dog it is vital to consult an expert.

When looking for a local trainer please ensure that they follow the guidelines that I have given here for behavior modification.

* Look for a kind trainer or behaviorist that uses careful and dog friendly methods to modify any unhelpful behavior that your dog has learned.

* Do your research and avoid anyone that wants to hurt, dominate or force train a dog. It will not work and will eventually make the behavior worse.

* Dog training and behavior is an unmodified profession therefore there are, surprisingly, a lot of self-proclaimed experts out there with no qualifications or scientific knowledge.

16) Some Additional Thoughts on Dog Training

As you will have probably gathered having read this far, dog training is a varied subject and one which has many myths. The main misconception that we see regularly, is that of dog and wolf pack logic, in short, dominance. To a certain extent, the following has been covered in the chapter on training. However, please find below additional information and information that is worth repeating.

a) What is the Dominance Theory?

Excessive dominance in dogs is a scientific theory which has been around for many years, and has really taken hold of our dog interactions.

Way back in the 1930s and 1940s Swiss animal behaviorist Rudolph Schenkel created a very specific environment where wolves were pushed together in a group; not of their choosing, and then observed.

There was a lot of friction in the group because wolves live as families and wild wolves do not simply choose a group and move in. Fences added to the friction and aggressive behavior ensued.

Dominance theory has since been revoked, and proof to the contrary has been developed. Yet people, usually uneducated dog trainers, still state that dominance within the pack, is the cause of all unhelpful dog behaviors. This type of trainer states that we must establish dominance over our family dogs in order for them to behave nicely. It is true, as you have read about certain behavior issues, that our dogs wish to please us and will do anything for our attention. So if we are dominant and are harsh towards a dog they will realize something is wrong and wish to correct this with passive, compliant behavior.

b) How Do Dominant Dog Trainers Work?

Establishing dominance as advised by dog trainers that practice the theory, involves the act of taking control of the dog's behavior. This is the same approach that the leader of a wolf pack would take towards an unruly member of the group. It is often stated as 'being an alpha'.

This would involve physical manipulation, ignoring the dog on greeting and going through doors first. It would also involve forcing, rather than training a dog to behave in a certain way.

There is another good reason for stepping away from the dominance theory. Dogs are not wolves. Although dogs descend from and are therefore genetically related to wolves, the existing genes carry a very small percentage of the inherent wolf. For over twenty thousand years, dogs and wolves have evolved separately.

Their behavior has evolved away from each other. Therefore by practicing this theory we are treating dogs like wolves. They are not, and in addition, we are assuming that captive wolves behave the same way as those living naturally in the wild.

Luckily the dog behavior world is evolving too. We are making changes based upon the study of actual dog behavior. So, with our increasing knowledge, this type of 'dominance theory' thinking should eventually become obsolete.

c) What is the alternative?

The other form of dog training I have previously mentioned is 'positive reinforcement training', and this is undoubtedly, the one which I favor. It is based upon careful understanding and study of dogs as the species they are.

So if you are looking for further help from a dog trainer, it is vitally important that you check credentials and methods, as not all dog trainers know the truth about dogs.

CHAPTER FIFTEEN:

CARING FOR YOUR SENIOR VIZSLA

When you first bring home your Vizsla puppy, it's difficult to imagine that in only 12 or 14 years later, you will have to say goodbye.

1) The Senior Vizsla

All dog breeds approach old age in the same way, but at different times, depending on their breed and size. Smaller dog breeds tend to live longer. Some dog breeds are still jumping agility courses at 13 years of age. Again, depending on the size, many other purebred dogs may only live to 8 or 9 years of age. Keep in mind that good health begins during puppy-hood and lasts a lifetime.

Your Vizsla has most likely been your best friend for life. You've both shared so many experiences. Your Vizsla will depend on you throughout his life. You've made a commitment to take care of him from puppy-hood to the end. Keep in mind that your Vizsla will change as he ages. His body and natural exuberance may sometimes allow you to forget his age. Then one day you'll look into your Vizsla's eyes and notice his silvery face, and stiffened gait. He'll most likely sleep longer, and may be less eager to play. As your Vizsla nears his ten-year mark, he'll start slowing down on his walks. Getting your Vizsla to live comfortably during his senior years need not be a challenge, but needs to be well-prepared for.

A) Caring for your Senior Vizsla

Most Vizslas will show signs of slowing down by graying of the coat and usually around the eyes and face. They will have a flaky coat, loss of hair, slowness of gait and enjoying the family couch more than usual. Activities like running, jumping, eating and retrieving will become more difficult for him. That said, other activities like sleeping, barking, and a repetition of habits may increase. Your Vizsla will want to spend more time with you, and will go to the front door more often when you are leaving.

As your Vizsla ages, he'll need certain therapeutic and medical preventative strategies. Your veterinarian will advise you on special nutritional counseling, veterinary visits and screening sessions for your senior Vizsla. A senior-care Vizsla program will include all of these.

Veterinarians will determine your Vizsla's health by doing blood smears for a complete blood count, which will include the following:

* Serum chemistry profile with electrolytes
* Urinalysis
* Blood pressure check
* Electrocardiogram
* Ocular tonometry (pressure of the eyeball)
* Dental prophylaxis

Extensive screenings for senior Vizslas is recommended well before dog owners begin to see the symptoms of aging, such as slower movement and disinterest in play and other activities.

By following this preventative program, you will not only increase your Vizsla's chance of a longer life, but you'll also make his life so much more comfortable. There will be so many physical changes like loss of sight through cataracts, arthritis, kidney problems, liver failure, and other possible degenerative diseases. Adding to that you may notice some behavioral changes related to aging. Vizslas suffering from hearing and eyesight loss, dental pain or arthritis may often become aggressive because of the constant pain that they have to live with. Vizslas that are near deaf or blind may also be startled more easily at the slightest environmental changes. Do your best not to move furniture around in your home, and to keep things as they are, as this can be unsettling for them. Senior Vizslas suffering from senility may do many unusual things, and will often become impatient.

B) House Soiling Accidents

These are associated with loss of bladder control, kidney problems, loss of mobility, loss of sphincter control, physiological brain changes, and reaction to new medications. Your older Vizsla will need more support than ever, especially doing his toilet business.

Avoid feeding your senior Vizsla too many unhealthy treats. Obesity is a common problem in older dogs as they naturally become less active. Additional weight will put extra stress on his joints and his body's vital organs. Some breeders suggest supplementing meals with high fiber foods that are also low in calories. You can also ask your veterinarian for a special prescription diet that best suits the needs of your senior Vizsla.

C) Every Day Tips

* Never punish or use harsh tones against your senior Vizsla for anything at all.

* Protect your Vizsla, and foresee his reactions to any environmental changes.

* Pay special attention to his immediate needs such as going to the toilet, pain levels and eating habits.

* Older Vizslas may not be able to wait until morning to go outdoors. Provide him with alternatives such as puppy pads or spread out newspaper, to relieve himself on during the night/early hours.

* Visit your veterinarian often and work together on providing your senior Vizsla with the best of care.

* Keep your Vizsla company. Your Vizsla does not understand why he's losing his sight or hearing. The world may seem to be a strange place to him right now. Comfort him frequently, and try to leave a family member with him when you go out. Your Vizsla will appreciate the companionship.

Be consistent with your schedule and do not change the way things are in your home. Doors that have always remained open should stay that way. Leave his favorite couch in the same place.

d) Keeping a Diary

You may wish to keep a diary to note the day-to-day record of how your Vizsla is feeling and whether he is eating, drinking and walking. As a dog owner you are able to observe all your Vizsla's activities, and record how your Vizsla feels and behaves.

e) Check list of questions about your aging Vizslas condition

* Is your Vizsla still happy to see you and how does he respond? Is it with his usual wag or does he seem to be less responsive than normal?

* Does he still come to you when called? What is his reaction to your being there? Record the levels of anxiety and pain. When he wags his tail or walks to you.

* Can your Vizsla still walk? Does he still get up and come to you? How far can he walk until he tires?

* Record his respiratory rate each evening when your Vizsla is resting peacefully. Record the breaths taken per minute.

* How much pain does your Vizsla seem to have? Does he have many episodes of pain? Does he yelp when handled or display signs of aggression when handled?

* Does your Vizsla eat if presented with his favorite foods? Does your Vizsla pick at his food or refuse to try some?

* Weigh your Vizsla every day or every week. If he is losing weight, how much weight is your Vizsla losing each week or month? Weight is an important indicator of health.

* Does your Vizsla still drink fluids? How much fluid per day/week. Dog owners can measure fluid intake per day.

* Is your Vizsla defecating, and how often does this occur? Are all his feces normal?

* Is any disease/illness worsening or improving?

F) Is There An Emergency Health Deterioration Stage?

Your Vizsla could suffer from an acute situation that is related to their condition. These chronic or acute episodes of disease related deterioration require immediate veterinary treatment. Some internal cancers will present themselves with hemorrhaging and states of severe shock and collapse. Congestive heart failure results in distressed breathing and pulmonary edema. Vizslas with renal failure, for example, will start vomiting blood and go into shock.

G) Symptoms of Pain in Your Senior or Terminally Ill Vizsla

It is always devastating when medical treatment does not work. But it's also important to think about the potential suffering of your Vizsla and how he was before the illness or injury. So as to determine whether your Vizsla is in pain or not, veterinarians and most importantly Vizsla owners need to have a way to determine a Vizslas' pain and pain threshold.

Typical symptoms are as follows:

* Whimpering, whining and yelping when touched.

* Your Vizsla yelps when he tries to get from point A to point B.

* Your Vizsla is often depressed, and does not want to interact with other animals or people in the household.

* Sleeplessness, listlessness and hiding under the bed or in dark places.

* Your Vizsla has an elevated heart rate.

* Your Vizsla injures himself by attacking or injuring the pain inflicted area.

* Chattering of the teeth is suggestive of mouth pain and dental pain, but is also indicative of shock, overall trauma and pain throughout the body.

* Your Vizsla is drooling excessively. This is suggestive of pain and trauma.

* Your Vizsla is squinting which is typical for head and eye pain in animals. Some dogs will squint both eyes when experiencing head pain.

2) Time To Say Goodbye!

If you are lucky, those 10 to 12 years or so, are what you get; a number of years that feel so very short. Nonetheless, mercifully, although we are aware of the unfair discrepancy between our dogs' lifespan and ours, we always somehow manage to push aside this fact; that is, until we are facing the very end with our dogs.

The heartbreaking decision to "put down" or euthanize your dog is an issue frequently faced by pet parents and veterinarians. You will never be prepared for this day. Putting your Vizsla to sleep is an extremely difficult and upsetting decision that you will need to make with your veterinarian. As a Vizsla owner, you will usually be making this decision when your Vizsla goes through one or more life-threatening symptoms that will force you to seek veterinary help immediately.

If the prognosis indicates that the end is near and that your Vizsla is in great pain, euthanasia may be the right choice. It is a difficult and heartbreaking decision for any dog lover. But if the dog is suffering then it is cruel to prolong their agony.

3) What is Euthanasia?

Just the thought of euthanasia or putting our Vizsla to sleep is enough to make anyone cringe. There are varying opinions about this final decision. What are the rights and wrongs? Are we actually helping our dogs or being selfish? Do we have the right to end a life?

Euthanasia refers to the planned and painless death of a dog that is suffering from a painful condition, or who is old and cannot walk, cannot see or unable to control his bodily functions. It is usually done with an overdose of an anesthesia.

The process of euthanasia takes a matter of seconds. Once the injection takes place it quickly enters the blood stream and the dog goes to sleep. The overdose suppresses the heart and brain function, in turn causing an instant loss of consciousness and therefore, pain. The animal dies peacefully while asleep.

The difficult decision to euthanize your senior or sick Vizsla is never an easy one, and one that may take a while for you to come to terms with. This time is usually stressful for you and your family. If this is a first time in dealing with the death of a loved one, you'll need your family by you.

4) What Happens Afterwards?

I know many vets who will give the owner of their beloved pet, the option to take them away and bury them in a quiet area of their garden. This may well be a favorite spot that their Vizsla frequented. You are generally advised to dig a hole deep enough to avoid the problem of foxes or similar predators, digging the body up.

If your Vizsla is buried in a pet cemetery, or in your yard, it's also a good idea to plant a special tree or stone over the site. A few dog owners prefer to leave their deceased dogs at the veterinary clinic. Today, many pet parents opt for individual cremation. Your veterinarian can help to arrange the cremation service, and will also be able to advise you on where to find a suitable pet cemetery.

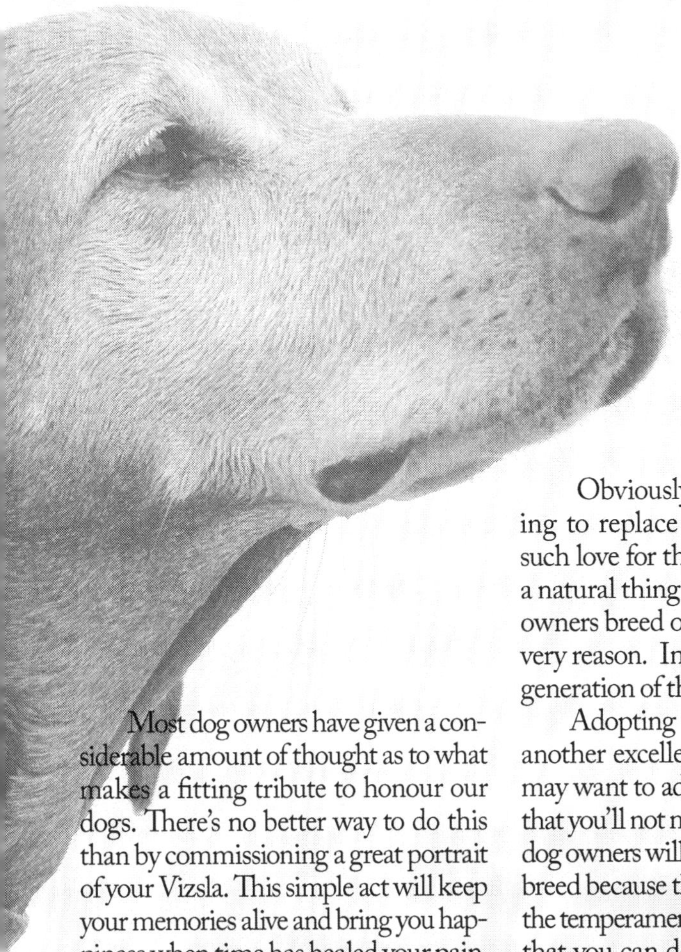

Most dog owners have given a considerable amount of thought as to what makes a fitting tribute to honour our dogs. There's no better way to do this than by commissioning a great portrait of your Vizsla. This simple act will keep your memories alive and bring you happiness when time has healed your pain. After spending nearly a decade together sharing life's most special moments, you'll be able to recall your Vizsla's most happy, crazy and sometimes most peaceful moments with a portrait. Professional studio photos are also a great alternative to this. After some time you may miss not having your friend around. You may perhaps wish to give a loving home to another Vizsla.

Obviously you are not attempting to replace your friend, but have such love for the breed that this seems a natural thing to consider. Many dog owners breed one litter of pups for this very reason. In that way they keep the generation of their beloved dogs intact.

Adopting a Vizsla from a rescue is another excellent option. Perhaps you may want to adopt a different breed so that you'll not make comparisons. Most dog owners will usually choose the same breed because they understand and love the temperament. Perhaps the best thing that you can do for yourself as well as your departed Vizsla will be to adopt another Vizsla.

" If there are no dogs in heaven, then when I die I want to go where they went."

-Will Rogers

CHAPTER SIXTEEN:

VIZSLA CARE SHEET

In reading this book you have received a wealth of information on the Vizsla breed. When you bring your Vizsla puppy home, you may have questions or you might want to reference a key piece of information from this book. Rather than flipping through the entire book you can use this care sheet to find the most important Vizsla facts about the breed, its nutritional needs, habitat requirements and breeding.

1.) Basic Breed Information

Pedigree: ancestors were hunting dogs of the Magyar tribes living in the Carpathian Basin during the 10th century

Breed Size: medium

Height (male): 22 to 25 inches (56-64 cm)

Height (female): 21 to 24 inches (53 to 61 cm)

Weight (male): 45 to 66 lbs. (20 to 30 kg)

Weight (female): 40 to 55 lbs. (18 to 25 kg)

Coat Length: short and close-lying

Coat Texture: smooth and dense; no woolly undercoat. The wirehaired is obviously rougher and courser

Color: solid golden-rust; dark mahogany or pale yellow are considered faults

Markings: some small white markings on the forehead, chest, neck, and tail are permissible

Eyes and Nose: reddish; eye, nose, and nail color should blend with the coat color

Ears: drop ears; very thin leather

Tail: very long; usually docked at two-thirds length

Temperament: high-energy, loyal, well-mannered, affectionate and intelligent.

Training: intelligent and extremely trainable

Exercise Needs: fairly high; long daily walk or jog recommended; breed is likely to develop problem behaviors without adequate mental/physical stimulation

Lifespan: average 10 to 14 years

Heath Conditions: hip dysplasia, canine epilepsy, lymphoma, hemangiosarcoma, and sebaceous adenitis

2.) Habitat Requirements

Indoor/Outdoor: indoor only

Necessary Accessories: crate, dog bed, food/water dishes, toys, collar, leash, grooming supplies

Collar and Leash: sized by weight

Grooming Supplies: shedding blade, gentle dog-friendly shampoo, toenail clippers,

Grooming Frequency: brush several times a week; professional grooming every 6 months

Exercise Requirements: daily walk plus playtime

Crate: highly recommended

Crate Size: just large enough for dog to lie down and turn around comfortably

Crate Extras: lined with blanket or plush pet bed

Food/Water: stainless steel bowls, clean daily

Toys: start with an assortment, see what the dog likes; include some mentally stimulating toys

3.) Nutritional Information

Nutritional Needs: water, protein, carbohydrate, fats, vitamins, minerals

RER: 30 x (weight in kg) + 70

Calorie Needs: varies by age, weight, and activity level; RER modified with activity level

Amount to Feed (puppy): feed freely but consult recommendations on the package

Amount to Feed (adult): consult recommendations on the package; calculated by weight

Important Ingredients: fresh animal protein (chicken, beef, lamb, turkey, eggs), digestible carbohydrates (rice, oats, barley), animal fats

Important Minerals: calcium, phosphorus, potassium, magnesium, iron, copper and manganese

Important Vitamins: Vitamin A, Vitamin B-12, Vitamin D, Vitamin C

Look For: AAFCO statement of nutritional adequacy; protein at top of ingredients list; no artificial flavors, dyes, preservatives

Quality Formulas: Nutro Natural Choice – High Endurance Adult Dog Food; Breeder's Choice Active Care Healthy Joint Dog Food; Earthborn Holistic Primitive Natural Dry Dog Food; Performatrin Ultra Grain-Free Dry Dog Food

4.) Breeding Information

Age of First Heat: around 6 months

Breeding Age: about 12 months; not during the first heat

Heat (Estrus) Cycle: 14 to 21 days

Frequency: twice a year, every 6 to 7 months

Greatest Fertility: 11 to 15 days into the cycle

Gestation Period: 59 to 63 days

Pregnancy Detection: possible after 21 days, best to wait 28 days before veterinary examination

Feeding Pregnant Dogs: maintain normal diet until week 5 or 6 then slightly increase rations

Signs of Labor: body temperature drops below normal 100° to 102°F (37.7° to 38.8°C), may be as low as 98°F (36.6°C); dog begins nesting in a dark, quiet place

Contractions: period of 10 minutes in waves of 3 to 5 followed by a period of rest

Whelping: puppies are born in 1/2 hour increments following 10 to 30 minutes of forceful straining

Puppies: born with eyes and ears closed; eyes open at 3 weeks, teeth develop at 10 weeks

Litter Size: average 6 to 8 puppies

Size at Birth: 14 to 20 ounces

Weaning: start offering puppy food soaked in water at 6 weeks; fully weaned by 8 weeks

Socialization: start as early as possible to prevent puppies from being nervous as an adult

Chapter Seventeen:

Relevant Websites & Conclusion

In reading this book you have received a wealth of information about the Vizsla breed and its care. As you prepare to become a Vizsla owner yourself you will need to stock up on supplies including food, toys, a crate, and other accessories. To help you find high-quality supplies for your Vizsla, check out some of the relevant websites in this chapter. You will find links to relevant websites for Vizsla food, Vizsla toys, Vizsla crates and dog beds, and other Vizsla accessories.

1.) FOOD FOR VIZSLA DOGS

Providing your Vizsla with a healthy diet is the key to maintaining good health. In this section you will find a collection of relevant websites for Vizsla food.

United States Links:

"High Endurance Adult Dog Food." Nutro Natural Choice. http://www.nutro.com/natural-dog-food/nutro/dry/high-endurance-3020-chicken-meal-whole-brown-rice-oatmeal-recipe.aspx

"Active Care Healthy Joint Formula." Breeder's Choice. http://www.goactivedog.com/

"Pedigree Active Targeted Nutrition with Chicken, Rice and Vegetables." Pedigree. http://www.pedigree.com/really-good-food/active-nutrition-for-dogs.aspx

"Which Dog Food is Right for My Dog?" SelectSmart.com. http://www.selectsmart.com/dogfood/

United Kingdom Links:

"Active – Chicken and Rice." Burns Natural Food for Pets. http://burnspet.co.uk/products/burns-for-dogs/dog-food-for-active-dogs.html

"Taste of the Wild Dog Food." Taste of the Wild. http://www.tasteofthewildpetfood.co.uk/

"Field & Trial – For Working and Active Dogs." Skinner's. http://www.skinnerspetfoods.co.uk/our-range/working-dogs/

"VetSpec Active Nutritional Supplement." VetSpec for Dogs. http://www.vetspec.co.uk/shop/vetspec-active-500g/

"Active and Working Dog Food." PetPlanet.co.uk. http://www.petplanet.co.uk/category.asp?dept_id=462

2.) CRATES AND BEDS FOR VIZSLA DOGS

Your Vizsla's crate is the place where he can retreat if he wants a nap or to take a break. In this section you will find a collection of relevant websites for dog crates and beds.

United States Links:

"Crates, Carriers & Pens." Drs. Foster and Smith. http://www.drsfostersmith.com/dog-supplies/dog-cages-crates-carriers-pens/ps/c/3307/10627

"Dog Beds." Cabela's. http://www.cabelas.com/browse.cmd?categoryId=463708080&WT.mc_id=ir10306&WT.tsrc=AFF&rid=10&irgwc=1

"Crates." PetSupplies.com. http://www.petsupplies.com/dog-supplies/crates/9113/

"Crates, Gates and Containment." PetsMart. http://www.petsmart.com/dog/crates-gates-containment/cat-36-catid-100013United Kingdom Links:

"Orvis Dog Beds." Orvis United Kingdom. http://www.orvis.co.uk/dog-beds#close

"Dog Crates." PetPlanet.co.uk. http://www.petplanet.co.uk/category.asp?dept_id=771

"Dog Crates and Kennels." Amazon.co.uk. http://www.amazon.co.uk/dog-kennel/b?ie=UTF8&node=471442031

"Dog Crates." RSPCA.org.uk. http://www.rspca.org.uk/adviceandwelfare/pets/dogs/environment/crates

"Dog Beds and Bedding." Pet-Supermarket.co.uk. http://www.pet-supermarket.co.uk/Category/Dog_Supplies-Dog_Beds_Bedding

3.) Toys and Accessories for Vizslas

Having the right toys and accessories for your Vizsla is very important. In this section you will find a collection of relevant websites for Vizsla toys and accessories.

United States Links:

"Interactive Dog Toys." Petco. http://www.petco.com/N_22_101/Dog-Toys.aspx

"Dog Toys." Chewy.com. http://www.chewy.com/dog/toys-315

"Bowls & Feeders." PetSmart. https://www.petsmart.com/dog/bowls-feeders/cat-36-catid-100010

"Dog Toys." Drs. Foster and Smith. http://www.drsfostersmith.com/dog-supplies/dog-toys/ps/c/3307/3

United Kingdom Links:

"Dog Toys." PetPlanet.co.uk. http://www.petplanet.co.uk/dept.asp?dept_id=16

"Dog Feeding and Watering Supplies." Amazon.co.uk. http://www.amazon.co.uk/dog-feeding-watering/b?ie=UTF8&node=471392031

"Dog Toys." VetUK. http://www.vetuk.co.uk/dog-toys-c-439

"Toys." Battersea Dogs & Cats Home. http://www.battersea.org.uk/apex/webshopitems?pageId=405-dogtoys&a=dog&b=toys

"Dog Bowls & Feeders." Pet-Supermarket.co.uk. http://www.

pet-supermarket.co.uk/Category/Dog_Supplies-Dog_Bowls_Feeders

4.) General Dog Care Information

The key to being the best Vizsla owner you can be, is to learn everything there is to know about dog ownership. In this section you will find a collection of relevant websites about various aspects of dog ownership.

United States Links:

"Dog Care." ASPCA.org. https://www.aspca.org/pet-care/dog-care

"Pet Care Center: Dog." PetMD. http://www.petmd.com/dog/petcare

"Dog Care and Behavior Tips." The Humane Society of the United States. http://www.humanesociety.org/animals/dogs/tips/?referrer=https://www.google.com/

"Dog Diet and Nutrition." WebMD. http://pets.webmd.com/dogs/guide/diet-nutrition

United Kingdom Links:

"Dogs – Dog Welfare." RSPCA.org.uk. http://www.rspca.org.uk/adviceandwelfare/pets/dogs

"General Advice About Caring for Your New Puppy or Dog." The Kennel Club. http://www.thekennelclub.org.uk/getting-a-dog-or-puppy/general-advice-about-caring-for-your-new-puppy-or-dog/

"Caring for the Older Dog." Blue Cross for Pets. http://www.bluecross.org.uk/pet-advice/caring-older-dog

"Caring for Dogs and Puppies." Battersea Dogs & Cats Home. http://www.battersea.org.uk/WEBShopItem?pid=01tb0000003JjxKAAS

"Dog Food Nutrition." Dog Breed Information Center. http://www.health-story.co.uk/dogbreedinfo/nutrition.htm

CONCLUSION

Hopefully you have read this far and have found the contents useful, informative and inspiring. There is a lot to consider when buying any dog, and consequently to appreciate their needs. Hopefully this book reflects that. For the most part, dogs that are properly looked after with love, care and respect, will repay you with unconditional love and devotion, many times over.

The intention of the book was not to overwhelm you the reader and put you off committing to being the guardian of this fantastic Vizsla breed. The intention was simply to give you as broad an appreciation as possible, so that you are fully prepared and equipped to properly look after and appreciate your new friend.

As you will realize, having read the various chapters, keeping a dog happy does not necessarily come without its problems. However, with correct awareness and training, many potential problems can be avoided. The health and welfare of your new Vizsla should go without saying, so please do everything you can to provide healthy food and a safe warm environment. In essence, it doesn't take a lot to keep your dog happy and healthy. At the very least you should be providing the following: (i) A warm safe habitat. (ii) Healthy food and fresh water, daily. (iii) Routine health procedures such as worming, flea treatment and veterinary check-ups. (iv) Basic training and regular daily exercise. (v) As much love and attention as you can provide.

Please remember that physical health can be counteracted by lack of mental stimulation. Whilst you can groom a dog all day long, thus pampering and giving him attention, if he doesn't get a free run, then he won't be truly happy.

Secondly it is vital to embrace scientific finding on the way your dog learns. In summary;

Dominance dog training is a myth that bypasses scientific findings on actual dog behavior. A dog learns from his environment and the attention, response that his own behavior provokes. This is positive reinforcement in action.

Punishment after a behavior will not make the behavior go away, because each time a behavior is carried out it is forming a habit. It is possible to mask an unhelpful behavior but it makes the dog feel bad and actually makes the behavior worse.

True behavior modification takes time and is carried out with kindness. The only true form of punishment to use is taking away attention when a behavior is problematic. This is called negative punishment and finally, our dogs do talk to us and we need to respect this by learning a little of their language.

Thank you for reading and allowing me to explain a little of what I know about your dog's mind and needs.

INDEX

O

P

R

S

T

U

V

W

Y

22587798R00115

Printed in Great Britain
by Amazon